THE
TREMULOUS
PRIVATE
BODY

The Anatomy Lesson by Rembrandt van Rijn; reproduced by permission of Mauritshuis, The Hague.

THE TREMULOUS PRIVATE BODY

Essays on Subjection

FRANCIS BARKER

Methuen

London and New York

First published in 1984 by
Methuen & Co. Ltd
11 New Fetter Lane, London EC4P 4EE

Published in the USA by
Methuen & Co.
in association with Methuen, Inc.
733 Third Avenue, New York, NY 10017

© 1984 Francis Barker

Printed in Great Britain
at the University Press, Cambridge
British Library Cataloguing in Publication Data
Barker, Francis
The tremulous private body.
1. English literature — Early modern,
1500-1700—History and criticism
I. Title
820.9'003   PR421
ISBN 0-416-37840-4
ISBN 0-416-37850-1 Pbk

Library of Congress Cataloging in Publication Data
Barker, Francis, 1952-
    The tremulous private body.

    1. English literature — Early modern, 1500-1700 —
History and criticism. 2. Body, human, in literature.
3. Art and literature. 4. Discourse analysis.
5. Mimesis.
I. Title.
PR429.B6B33 1984   820'.9'36 84-20754
ISBN 0-416-37840-4
ISBN 0-416-37850-1 (pbk.)

CONTENTS

PREFACE

I would like to record at the outset the use I have made of the work of others.

The passage from Pepys' *Diary* is quoted from the version in *John Evelyn and Samuel Pepys: Selections from the Diaries*, ed. James Gibson (London, 1957), pp.216-17. Line references against quotations from *Hamlet* refer to the New Cambridge Shakespeare text, ed. John Dover Wilson (Cambridge, 1936). Milton's *Areopagitica* is quoted from *The Works of John Milton*, gen. ed. Frank Allen Patterson, Vol. IV (New York, 1931). In the case of Descartes's *Discourse on Method* and *Meditations*, page numbers in the text, (D) or (M), refer to the edition translated and introduced by F. E. Sutcliffe (Harmondsworth, 1968). (I would also like to mention in this context my colleague Jay Bernstein whose teaching introduced me to Descartes and some of whose arguments I have reproduced.)

Any account of Rembrandt's first *Anatomy Lesson* must

be indebted to William S. Heckscher's remarkable 'iconological' study of the painting, *Rembrandt's Anatomy of Dr. Nicolaas Tulp* (New York, 1958) to which page numbers (*H*) refer. In my own reading of the canvas (pp.73-85), and on p.115, I have drawn freely on that work for information, and occasionally points of interpretation also.

I mention on p.49 the MS account book known commonly as *Henslowe's Diary*, which so troubles in its empirical way traditional versions of the relationship between author and text. It can be consulted in Walter W. Greg's edition in two parts, *Text* (London, 1904) and *Commentary* (London, 1908).

Christopher Hill's remarks on the pastoral and censorship, which I make use of on p.51, are in his *Milton and the English Revolution* (London, 1979), pp.50-1; on p.88 I refer to his reading of Marvell; see 'Society and Andrew Marvell' in *Puritanism and Revolution* (London, 1958), p.348.

The reference on p.18 to Russian formalism and the concept of motivation can be followed up, in the first instance, by reference to Viktor Shklovsky's paper 'Art as technique', in Lee T. Lemon and Marion J. Reis, *Russian Formalist Criticism: Four Essays* (Lincoln, Neb., 1965), pp.3-24; and beyond this in Victor Erlich, *Russian Formalism: History-Doctrine* (The Hague, 1980).

On p.18 is a reference to Bertolt Brecht whose attack, in theory and in theatre practice, on bourgeois naturalism lies behind some of my remarks on Jacobean drama. Brecht's work can be usefully approached through J. Willett, *Brecht on Theatre: The Development of an Aesthetic* (London, 1964).

For Walter Benjamin's theory of history, to which I allude on p.21, see initially his 'Theses on the philosophy of history', in *Illuminations*, trans. Harry Zohn, edited and introduced by Hannah Arendt (London, 1973). See further his philosophical and critical work on the seventeenth century *Trauerspiel*, *The Origin of German Tragic Drama*, trans. John Osborne (London, 1977). For a sustained meditation on Benjamin, see Terry Eagleton, *Walter Benjamin or Towards a Revolutionary Criticism* (London, 1981).

For the notion of the British constitution being never written in fact but always 'inscribed elsewhere' I am indebted to Colin Mercer's work on Hobbes, which to the best of my knowledge as yet remains unpublished.

For Freud's 1901 analysis of Dora, and her eventual refusal to which I allude first on p.57, see his 'case history', *Fragment of an Analysis of a Case of Hysteria*, in *The Standard Edition of the Complete Psychological Works of Sigmund Freud*, gen. ed. James Strachey (London, 1953-74), Vol. VII. On p.108 and elsewhere I refer to Freud's notion of the death drive; for this see *Beyond the Pleasure Principle* [1920], ibid., Vol. XVIII, and *Civilisation and its Discontents* [1930], ibid., Vol. XXI.

And for Lacan's, sometimes lucid, re-reading of Freud (p.57) see principally his *Écrits*, trans. Alan Sheridan (London, 1977). This volume includes (pp.8-29) the paper on 'aggressivity' which I refer to on p.89: 'Aggressivity in psychoanalysis'.

The reference on p.58 to R. D. Laing is to his *The Divided Self* (Harmondsworth, 1965).

There is an allusion to Louis Althusser's theory of interpellation on p.59; for this see his 'Ideology and ideological state apparatuses', *Lenin and Philosophy and Other Essays*, trans. Ben Brewster (London, 1971). Althusser's remarks on the 'simplest' acts of existence are cited from his 'From *Capital* to Marx's philosophy', in Louis Althusser and Étienne Balibar, *Reading Capital*, trans. Ben Brewster (London, 1975), p.16.

My mention on p.104 of Georg Lukács is intended to refer to his 'Reification and the consciousness of the proletariat', in *History and Class Consciousness*, trans. Rodney Livingstone (London, 1971), pp.83-222.

Pierre Macherey's borrowing of Spinoza's idea of the ardent life, which I in turn employ on p.110, is in his *A Theory of Literary Production*, trans. Geoffrey Wall (London, 1978), p.63.

My most pervasive theoretical debt is probably to the enormously suggestive work on discourse, power and the body carried out by Michel Foucault. I refer to it explicitly on p.13, but, despite particular points of disagreement and my sense of the political inadequacy of many of his formulations – especially on 'power' – his 'influence' on my text is widespread. See his *Madness and Civilisation: A History of Insanity in the Age of Reason*, trans. Richard Howard (London, 1971); *Discipline and Punish: The Birth of the Prison*, trans. Alan Sheridan (London, 1977); also *The History of Sexuality*, Vol. I, trans. Robert Hurley (London, 1979). I should also point out that the passage from Descartes's *Meditations* quoted on pp.60-1 has been the subject of some debate between Foucault and Jacques Derrida. It was originally interpreted by Foucault, along lines followed in the present text, in his *Histoire de la folie* (Paris, 1961), although in a passage regrettably not included in the English version of that book, *Madness and Civilisation*. Derrida attacked Foucault's reading of Descartes in 'Cogito and the history of madness'; see his *Writing and Difference*, trans. Alan Bass (London, 1978). For Foucault's reply to Derrida, first published as an appendix to the second (1972) edition of the *Histoire*, see 'My body, this paper, this fire', trans. Geoff Bennington, *The Oxford Literary Review*, 4, 1, Autumn 1979, pp.9-28.

It is, of course, the work of Jacques Derrida that has conducted the most sustained questioning of the phonocentric 'metaphysics of presence' and posited thereby the death in writing of the subject; I recall the thematic outline of that interrogation on p.106 and *passim*, and adopt some of Derrida's language. See principally his *Of Grammatology*, trans. Gayatri Chakravorty Spivak (Baltimore, 1976); and *Writing and Difference*.

A number of people and institutions have helped me materially and intellectually with the production of this book. I wish particularly to mention the following and to thank them. The University of Essex gave me study-leave in which to write, and a research grant from the Department of Literature made it possible for me to see Rembrandt's *Anatomy Lesson*. Pernille Petersen's contribution has been incalculable throughout and is deeply appreciated. I would also like to thank Catherine Belsey for her encouragement, for many stimulating discussions, and for her detailed criticism of the manuscript. Antony Easthope and Jonathan White both read a part of the manuscript and commented critically and supportively. Jean Poynter and Sylvia Sparrow typed it excellently against the clock.

Marijn van Rooij helped prepare the text for publication; I am grateful to her for this and much besides.

And for their unfailing patience and sustaining friendship I thank especially Peter Hulme and Diana Loxley to whom this book is dedicated.

Francis Barker,
Spring, 1984.

A
CHALLENGED
SPECTACLE

Rosencrantz. My lord, you must tell us where the
         body is, and go with us to the king.
Hamlet. The body is with the king. . .

(Hamlet)

February 9th (Lord's day). Up, and at my chamber all the morning and the office doing business, and also reading a little of *L'escholle des filles*, which is a mighty lewd book, but yet not amiss for a sober man once to read over to inform himself in the villainy of the world. At noon home to dinner, where by appointment Mr. Pelling come and with him three friends, Wallington, that sings the good base, and one Rogers, and a gentleman, a young man, his name Tempest, who sings very well indeed, and understands anything in the world at first sight. After dinner we went into our dining-room, and there to singing all the afternoon. (By the way, I must remember that Pegg Pen was bought to bed yesterday of a girl; and among other things, if I have not already set it down, that hardly ever was remembered such a season for the smallpox as these last two months have been, people being seen all up and down the streets, newly come out after the smallpox.) But though they sang fine things, yet I must confess that I did take no pleasure in it, or very little, because I understood not the words, and with the rests that the words are set, there is no sense nor understanding in them though they be English, which makes me weary of singing in that manner, it being but a worse sort of instrumental musick. We sang until almost night, and drank a mighty good store of wine, and then they parted, and I to my chamber, where I did read through *L'escholle des filles*, a lewd book, but what do no wrong once to read for information sake. And after I had done it I burned it, that it might not be among my books to my shame, and so at night to supper and to bed. (*The Diary of Samuel Pepys*, entry for 9 February 1668)

The scene of writing and of reading, is, like the grave, a private place. We must explore the contents of this privacy, in relation to what is publicly speakable, and draw the diagram of the structure of confessions and denials of desire that gives this passage its peculiar numinosity, and, in principle, as a representative, a special place in history of the bourgeois soul.

In Pepys' chamber, unlike the quiet tomb in which the dismembered but visible body of Marvell's beloved was recently interred, if not echoing songs, at least ghostly mutterings can indeed be heard, rustling among the feints and side-steps of the text's involuted speech. Where in Marvell's poem sex was the objective, publicly invoked and celebrated, and death the price of its refusal, here we have entered a different, secluded domain to which sex has been banished; a silent bedroom, traversed by whispers which intimate – of necessity, obliquely – a sexuality which cannot any longer be frankly avowed.

The discourse of the Navy Office clerk is, no doubt, attenuated. That is part of its charm and is certainly the stylistic register which has characterized its reproduction and transmission in the history of writing. Not too verbose, barely literary; after all that rhetoric that preceded it, a breath of fresh air. With the verbal excess of the Renaissance behind us, not to say *sotto voce* those other excesses of the recent revolution, we emerge at last into a clear, known world of facts and events, of business and leisure, and into a discourse appropriate to that world. A discourse shorn of its ornaments; a plain style for our bourgeois times. At least, this is how we have been taught to read Pepys' text by those commentators who have identified its significances for us in a way characterized by nothing so much as a plainness, an obviousness given in the image of a mind writing down mundane events according to the clear order of their unfolding, providing a text whose regularities, it is said, are determined only by the pattern of the empirical, whose transcription it is. 'Up, and at my chamber all the morning and at the office doing business.' This is the discourse we have learned to read, which in its unalterable presence leaves us strictly nothing to say. Nothing further can be said. Everything is here and now, perceived and written down. What is beyond perception is never paused over. The text is not a fiction and cannot thus be criticized. We have been trained to read in silence, fixed by its light, taut factuality –

by a small technique of sensibility rather than a grand gesture of power – into the inexorable domain of the quotidian real.

And we have acceded in this discourse to a social reality which is, whatever dangers it may hold, essentially simple. It is here, there, given, waiting to be written down. Clarified already in its common-sense existence, life needs only the perceiving mind and the writing hand, tracing and recording its contours, to become text. The apparency of the bourgeois world and its texts is born.

There is probably a good deal to be said about what might be called the conservative value of discovering and promulgating this description of the discourse of the clerk. Especially important would be the way in which the text, or at least the assumptions governing the reading of it here cited, might come to stand in for discourse itself, for all discourse, and would then function to abolish not only the history of style that precedes it, but all history, the aura of its relative antiquity enticing us to become knowing enough to smile at its little proprieties and to appreciate in the world it reflects those picturesque differences that momentarily block, and thus freshen, our recognition of how like our own world it really is. Don't plainness of style and the epistemological naïvety it suggests thus function as a guarantee of profound identity, allowing us across a gulf which we call history but which by the very nature of this particular claim to intelligibility is nothing more than the deployment of sameness along a chronological axis, to glimpse and embrace in Pepys, the 'man' rather than the text, the duration and durability of the affections, pleasures, discontents and even – let us not be too superior even in our admissions of equality – the petty vanities which are truly our own? Textual good sense would come to dominate not only the rightness of the world's appearances, but also the inexorability of the domain of time itself; the sign, in other words, of a radical incapacity for essential change.

Yet, for all that, the plain style works as a mask, or at best a detour, for both Pepys, the 'I' that writes and is written, and for the commentators who have reconstructed what turns out to be so little of him. The material history of the text

5

ought to provide a converse image of this mystificatory clarity. A text ciphered and partly coded, hidden in a difficult early seventeenth-century shorthand, written in secret and kept locked away during Pepys' lifetime (and him driven blind by it), bequeathed, lost for so long a period to the *public* domain. Against what odds of obscurity has all this imputed transparency been achieved. And at what risk, or perhaps promise, of truncation of the bourgeois soul it has come to represent.

It is most signally in the practice of writing advanced by the text itself that this foreshortening is achieved. The passage deploys two recensions of the same alibi on either side of an interpolation which is, in part, parenthesized. Perhaps this is the typical structure of all bourgeois discourse? At any rate, the a-libi-dinous justification of reading 'for information sake' belongs properly to what has been called hitherto the discourse of the clerk, and no doubt also provides, in general if not actually by the local authority of these particular lines, the basis for the informational mode of reading that has characterized the reception of Pepys' text.

But what is remarkable here is not the relative lack of opacity of the self-deception (to and for whom is Pepys writing this secret text?) but the indirect, if none the less urgent, manner of its self-exposure in another discourse within and around that of the clerk. Unspeakable in their 'proper' place, the pleasures of the lewd text, *L'escholle des filles*, surface, and are in turn denied, elsewhere; in confessions and disavowals apparently disconnected from their real source, the guilty reading; yet forever connected back to it by the sign of their very excess over the textual motivations which only apparently justify their actual disposition in the passage.

So, the proposition that Pepys reads the lewd text over 'to inform himself in the villainy of the world' (the grammatical third person is significant, as if, which is the case, he is trying to speak of someone else, another self, although 'in' speaks eloquently if ambiguously of where Pepys already thinks he is in relation to the sin of the world) barely succeeds in even containing another discourse, one concerning desire,

6

disease, the mess of the body and its passions, that disrupts and intrudes upon the calm order of plain speech. In spite of the steps the discourse of the clerk takes to forestall these others, and of the fact that, arguably, this is its principal *raison d'être*, it nevertheless ruses with itself, and becomes self-treacherous.

In this way we can begin to understand the precision of verbal usage which otherwise looks erroneous. The item 'yet *I must confess* that I did take no pleasure in it', which purports to refer to a certain kind of singing that Pepys despises, provides an efficient instance. The whole passage is dominated by its initial 'Lord's day', which functions doubly: from an informational point of view it is a temporal mark – all the *Diary*'s Sundays are identified in this way – but discursively it is an admonition whose minatory value must be contained within the punctuational *cordon sanitaire* of the bracket within which it has been confined. But the insulation that separates the 'Lord's day' from the rest of the passage is not impervious to every kind of charge. While it serves effectively to permit the efficient pursuit of 'business' which is mentioned, unproblematically, in passing, it otherwise merely redoubles the anxiety associated with the lewd reading. So that when we come to Pepys' comment on his lack of enjoyment of the singing, a religious idiom is incited. Singing is perhaps bodily enough a practice to have given the right clues without such an overt confession of the need to confess. In any case, only truly Pepysian efforts of common sense, or informational reading, could avert the recognition that what is at stake here is the simultaneous admission and denial of the furtive pleasures of the French text, displaced onto an apparently innocuous, and, significantly, public and social pastime. By the same token, perhaps, the tongue loosened by alcohol has its part to play here. The 'sober man' of informational reading, the bourgeois citizen grave in the dignity of his public demeanour, is, we can now see, almost inevitably not just one who has drunk 'a mighty good store of wine', but one who must blurtingly confess himself to have done so.

The text employs massive means – not of repression, for

everything is said, eventually, even if it is not acknowledged as having been said – but of diversion: we are asked to look 'by the way' at 'other things'. But just as no amount of raucous singing by Pepys and his friends will ever drown out the loquaciousness of the half-silence in which the forbidden book is enjoyed, so, the more the text denies interest, diverts attention, only the more clearly does it identify its unacknowledged drives. No doubt, as the empiricist would have it, the parenthesis of smallpox and childbirth at the centre of the passage is simply part of the 'day's residue', faithfully noted by the honest recorder. But why these sentences, just here, deployed in quite this relation to the others? Can it be with total fortuitousness that Pepys speaks 'by the way' of a young woman 'brought to bed' in an idiom not only of childbirth but of sexuality (as if the connotative, and indeed material, connection were not explicit enough)? And to speak in the same breath of disease, dis-ease, an affliction punishing the body so loathed by Pepys, as by any sober man on the Lord's day, and moreover, a privatized affliction after which people are 'newly come out' to be 'seen all up and down the streets'. The connotative relations established here are clear: from the bedroom to the public scene; from sickness to health; from private, sick sexuality to sexless public health.

It is the same 'fortuitousness', which is uncanny but far from arbitrary, that governs what we are told of the quasi-mythical Mr Tempest. Envied for his class, his youth and his sexuality (we now know what the metaphor 'sings very well indeed' means), he is also feared for his perspicacity. Truly a tempest come to disturb the calm order of the bourgeois *domus*, a man who 'understands everything in the world at first sight', as if, a good sight-reader of music, his ability will flow over to penetrate the concealments and immediately see through to the hidden text with which Pepys pleasured himself that morning and which he will surely take to bed with him that night. It is because of the threat represented by Tempest that Pepys finally burns *L'escholle des filles*, to make finally sure. In the presence of such a seer it is not enough to hide the text, like the *Diary* itself, in layers of cipher and, at

8

the moments the language of prurience calls most 'frank', in a garble of foreign languages (see how Pepys *tells* his desire that the truth of his own text should not be read – 'I understood not the words . . . there is no sense nor understanding in them though they be English'), but all that guilt must be absolutely consumed by a cleansing, purifying fire. The smallpox of sexuality is to be cauterized by a sacred flame, just as London itself, visited for its sins by plague a few years earlier, is then purified by fire.

So. An image of a man. A typical man. A bourgeois man. Riven by guilt, silence and textuality. Forbidden to speak and yet incited to discourse, and therefore speaking obliquely in another place. Who says sing when he means fuck, who fears sex and calls it smallpox, who enjoys sex and calls it reading, who is fascinated and terrified by texts and so reads them once, but only for information's sake, who is sober and drunk. Who would rather burn his body, who would rather go blind, but who, as in the storm of rage with which he tears, elsewhere in the *Diary*, his wife's pathetic love-letters, obliterates the texts instead.

A representation of a representation, moreover. Behind it all, not even an adulterous act, but an act of reading. A lewd book.

*   *   *   *

The enclosure of the Pepysian moment is its decisive quality. The text itself rehearses the situation it discloses as it inlays seclusion within seclusion. The very writing, which as its epistemological principle grasps the outer world as an accessible transparency, recedes from that world towards an inner location where the soul – or, as the modern terminology has it, positionality in discourse – apparently comes to fill the space of meaning and desire. The boundaries of the outer context, designated as much by discourse as by a physical separation of space, are clearly defined, and the real energies and interests of the text then locate themselves within these frontiers. The diagram of the text is as a series of concentric circles at the furtive heart of which is the secret declivity of the soul itself. The I surrounded first by discourse, then by the *domus*, the chamber, and finally by the public world, is placed at the heart of its own empire, in silence and very largely in terror. The *Diary* for all the fullness of its days, despite being so richly populated with others and with the furniture of gossip and events, is thus the record of a terrible isolation. At the moment when the soul reaches out to appropriate the outer world, the very gesture reinforces the division by which it is other than what it seeks to apprehend. The obverse face of the reception of the *Diary* as a documentary record of the life and times of the Restoration is its status as an inner history, one of the first of the autobiographies in that tradition of subject-centred discourse which, as we shall see, Descartes began.

But despite its intimacy, Pepys' tormented situation is not peculiar to him but marks out a social condition which was novel at the time. In it, a complex of overdetermined relations coalesce, governing bourgeois subjectivity at its founding moment. By no means the tortured predicament of a single, aberrant individual – even its individuation is historically produced – this situation is the result of the revolutionary process that preceded it. The political upheaval of the mid-century established, as all revolutions must if they are to be thoroughgoing, a new set of connections between subject and discourse, subject and polity, and in doing so altered fundamentally the terms between which these mutually constitutive relations held. In the space of a relatively few years a new set of relations between state and citizen, body and soul, language and meaning, was fashioned. The older sovereignty of the Elizabethan period was disassembled, and in its place was established a conjunction of novel social spaces and activities, bound together by transformed lines of ideological and physical force, among which new images of the body and its passions were a crucial, if increasingly occluded, element. It is a history of this new emergence which is the concern of the present, intransitive, essay.

Having issued on to this situation, the historical process then appeared to drain itself away, effacing its own marks as

10

it hands the subject over to the depoliticized privacy newly marked out for it. But the outcome is none the less historical for the fact that a property of its historical form is an apparent dehistoricization of its own achievement. That Pepys is now located as a private citizen in a domestic space, over against a public world is not, thus, a natural fact, but merely one of the more grossly structural features of a historical settlement (however provisional, as are all historical situations) which the century acceded to by means of an extreme and often bloody effort. None of the main features of this settlement can be read as the sign of an eternal condition. The apparent directness of its profoundly evasive discourse; the apparent ease of access of its discourse, launched from an inner place, to an outer, clarified world; the guilty secrecy not only of its writing but of its sexuality; the privatization of its bodies and their passions; all are instances of a new ensemble of what can only be described as power relations, in so far as they designate a type and a locatedness for subjectivity and fix it *in place* among a new set of divisions, dominations, of the social formation constructed from and among the debris of the older regime. That they are recognizable in all their aspects today indicates the viability of the construction and need not tempt us to underestimate its novelty (nor, for that matter, to assume its permanence).

The context of the inauguration of Pepys' situation has already been extensively defined. The broad process of transition from the feudal to the capitalist mode of production (which, unlike the political transformation, cannot be dated with chronometric precision) and the rise of the modern state provide the general co-ordinates within which the reformulation of the subjectivity appropriate to them can be mapped. But what has been less frequently treated is the manner in which the grand historical process interpenetrates the detail of what until recently has been regarded as barely historical features of social life. The gross restructuring of a political system or a mode of economic production may even supply the explanatory basis for an understanding of the more intimate textures, but will remain

11

in any case abstract and incomplete unless that supplementary work of definition and evocation is carried out. In the long run the tragicomedy of the body and the soul may even prove decisive.

The Pepysian settlement, then, must be taken as a moment of definite importance not only for the ideological, economic and political history of the seventeenth century and its foundation of the modern situation, but also within the corporeal history of that establishment. We shall attempt to grasp the precise status of the body in that settlement below, but for the moment it is necessary to note the mere fact, for the body has certainly been among those objects which have been effectively hidden from history. Not least because one of the principal components of that establishment of the modern which the Pepysian situation signals is the very de-realization of the body which subsequent historiography has been heir to. When Hamlet – himself, as we shall see, on the threshold of modernity – called for this 'too too sullied flesh' to 'melt,/Thaw and resolve itself into a dew' (I.ii.129-30), the seventeenth century would soon take him at his word. The consequence is there to be read in Pepys. The passions and the anxiety of the discourse-text swirl around an apparent absence which is none the less always there, if never 'in person'.

If the new ensemble of terms and relations is established conjuncturally around a particular corporeal status, this is not because the body is the essential foundation of the structure. Not only would it be wrong to assign such ontological pre-eminence to any one moment in the ensemble, but it is a related and relational body which is at stake. However necessary it may be to isolate the body for analytic purposes, the body in question is not a hypostatized object, still less a simple biological mechanism of given desires and needs acted on externally by controls and enticements, but a relation in a system of liaisons which are material, discursive, psychic, sexual, but without stop or centre. It would be better to speak of a certain 'bodiliness' than of 'the body'. It is the instance of a suturing of discourse and desire to the organism (itself, of course, a historical

12

entity although subject to a longer, evolutionary, timespan in which today disease, diet and working conditions are the key determinants), and thus fully social in its being and in its ideological valency. Rather than an extra-historical residue, invariant and mute, this body is as ready for coding and decoding, as intelligible both in its presence and its absence, as any of the more frequently recognized historical objects. The site of an operation of power, of an exercise of meaning.

The work of description which has played the central part in opening up the possibility of a political history of the body is that carried out by Michel Foucault who traces the lineaments of the bourgeois order in studies of two of its essential components – the history of its madness and of its penality – and identifies there a transition, effected over a long period of time, from a socially visible object to one which can no longer be seen. It has its roots in the 'Great Confinement' of the seventeenth century which gathers into the new institutions of confinement that promulgated themselves throughout the whole of Europe during that century, the dispossessed elements of the population who were to become, for the new order, no more than a detritus. The sick, the poor, the orphaned, the homeless, the unemployed, the criminal and the mad, who had once been integrally present, were now, by an act of separation, first excluded from the scene, and then made useful. Within the houses of confinement they could be made to labour, and their labour regulated. The example was socially instructive, and their organized incarceration encoded symbolically and contributed in actuality to a complete restructuring of the social whole along new productive lines. The process matures in *l'âge classique* and is consummated in the nineteenth century with the global triumph of the bourgeois class.

Crucial to this transition was the relocation of the body. The scope of penality changes: the body involved in punishment, in spectacular, public, corporal pain, is removed into 'complete and austere institutions', where, within these closed and silent prisons, asylums and hospitals, it becomes the object – and at its most efficient, the subject –

of discipline. The central penal task is no longer to exact a recompense of pain, but to cure, by exemplary labour and other techniques, the prisoner's delinquent soul. She or he becomes the object of secret and overt surveillance rather than spectacular visibility. Technical measurement replaces the older art of judicial torture, and becomes the ground for the elaboration of the modern knowledges – penology, forensic psychiatry, *diagnosis* in all its medical and juridical forms – which are, for Foucault, instances of power in its contemporary form. From a precise violence of the body, to a precise knowledge of the modern soul; which is born, in Foucault's narrative, precisely in the moment of the disappearance of the body from public view; or, as the example of Pepys shows, at the moment when the very division between the public and the private is constructed in its modern form. It is thus that the pre-eminence of the soul in Pepys' text is predicated on, and a part of the history of, the body, newly banished from the sphere in which his troubled subjectivity now appears to be sovereign.

In pursuit of the decisive reshaping of the body politic and its subjectivity that was effected in the seventeenth century and which results in the Pepysian situation, it will be necessary to trace a path back across the years of the revolution, and to read in a text of Milton's and in the pervasive publicity of the Jacobean stage, the crisis of the older polity, and the main determinants of the outcome registered in Pepys and which in essential outline we have still to endure today. The historical settlement which preceded the bourgeois order of whose inner structure Pepys' predicament is an early instance, was profoundly different from that modernity of subjection which the revolution inaugurated. Only efforts of de-historicization similar to those practised by the Pepysian commentators, whose impressive but insidious simplicity we have already noticed, could hope to achieve even a partial assimilation of the pre-revolutionary to the present.

In particular the sign of the literary greatness of Shakespeare has played a major part in remaking the late feudal world in the image of the bourgeois settlement that grew up inside it, and eventually brought it down. If not the invariability of a quotidian discourse like that of the clerk, at least its more elevated version, the timelessness of great art, has had to be mobilized in order to secure the necesssary abolition of historical difference: Shakespeare's texts, their universality, their 'broad humanism' – even their beauty – have served, in the hands of left and right, to secure in an alien history a value and a point of reference by which the other can be identified as the same, and thus tamed, explained, and even appreciated.

This is not the place for an extensive critique of Shakespearian criticism or of the role of 'Shakespeare' in British culture, but the mere citation of the commanding position of the Shakespearian text within the reception of the pre-revolutionary discursivity will suffice to identify the order of difficulty to be encountered in trying to insist on the necessity of redrawing the map of that other world. In one sense, of course, all history is contemporary history, so what is at issue is not that Shakespeare's corpus has been re-produced in order to be reshaped to present needs: this is the general task of all historiography, and to believe otherwise would be to advance a hubristic objectivism. Nor is it necessary to deny that there are features in the Shakespearian text which lend themselves particularly well to the uses that have been found for them: this probably accounts for their 'greatness' in so far as the literary tradition has been able to celebrate what is, unknown to itself, a narcissistic self-confirmation, 'recognizing' in Shakespeare's transitional and contradictory *oeuvre* those elements which are truly its own. It is simply that another history must be written if our account of that corporal past is not to be merely a case of recapitulating in the pre-revolutionary texts the themes and structures which it was precisely the task of the revolution to establish, by *destroying* the polity whose complex index the Shakespearian discourse was.

The effort of historiographical denial of the situation for discourse and the body *abolished* by the Pepysian settlement is stamped on the other side of the coin of Shakespeare's present greatness: the minority of the other Jacobeans. Above all it is evident in the indictment for sensationalism which has so frequently secured the Jacobeans' inferior status in the calm and hygienic moral order that obtains in literary criticism, if nowhere else. In part, the charge of sensationalism goes to the substantive and recklessly bodily contents of the scenes and images that are said to elicit the sensation, and we shall return to them; but also, connected inextricably with this, it more covertly denigrates the Jacobean *mode* of representation itself, which is also alien to the history which succeeded it and the historiography which has refused its significance. The reception of the Jacobean text has proceeded in a fashion entirely subjugated to the partitive sign of the *literary* greatness of Shakespeare's verse: the word has found a place of privilege over the image. It is against this measure that a crux like that in which the Duchess of Malfi is shown the wax figures of the corpses – the bodies – of Antonio and his children by her tormentors, which is in essence spectacular although words are also spoken, has been judged in principle inferior to the kind so frequent in Shakespeare which is effected, allegedly, in language although accompanied by stage business. But what is at stake in opposing this organizing principle of the traditional reproduction of the Jacobean representational situation is not the banal plea for the 'living theatre' against the academicism of the play-*text*; still less is it designed to reinforce an existentially untenable opposition between word and image, and thus to enforce a spurious choice between them, but rather an assessment of the cost of this organization of the reception, recognizing the subsequent decisions that have been made regarding the relative weighting of language and spectacle within the historical retroaction of developments familiar to Pepys and his epoch, but not yet fulfilled in the theatre-world of the early seventeenth century.

Those who have attacked sensationalism would doubtless deny that they are carrying out the belated cultural work of the bourgeois revolution: but it is hard not to see in the attack on sensation the hand of a Protestant asceticism, and

16

in the demotion of the spectacle a continuity with the seventeenth century's own iconoclasm in favour of the Word. But then history has a way of working itself out behind the backs of its actors, as Marx pointed out. The potential for depravity of the moral sensibilities in the exercise of visual representation was an argument familiar to the period, and one repeatedly mobilized at the time against the liberty and the insistence of the visual in the Jacobean world theatre. It is thus not *necessary* to assume that a lack of goodwill, nor even an ignorant prejudice has governed the hierarchization of Shakespeare and 'the others'. Although it is true that the politics of a Middleton are more unacceptably radical, and that the reconciliatory complacency attempted by reaches of Shakespeare's discourse finds its critical opposite in the troubled, mordant sensibility of a Webster or a Tourneur, it is the more historical, and so more deeply political, rejection of the visibility of the mode of representation that controls the evaluations of the Jacobean texts as we receive them.

At the level of representation what has been elided – or acknowledged only in the condemnatory form of the charge of sensationalism – is the theatricality of this theatre, the innocent foregrounding of its device.

When a play like *The Revenger's Tragedy* cannot be regarded as particularly extraordinary for the fact that, almost without content and verging constantly on self-parody, it moves from one quoted stage device to another, we are clearly far from that occlusion of writing itself which is effected in the post-Pepysian world by the attribution to discourse of an instrumental transparency. Tourneur's text is constructed by tireless reference to its own signifying; each sequence is a matrix of citation, imitation and reworking of the range of theatrical tropes and mechanisms at work on the Jacobean stage, and in this sense is only a usefully typical example of the early seventeenth-century theatre as a whole. The masques and the masks, the quaint devices and the stereotyping of character and situation, the relentless artifice and even the all-pervasive metaphor of the theatre itself are not the exceptions to the rule of this theatre, but the rule itself. Even Shakespeare's writing culminates in *The Tempest*, that spectacle which has been criticized so frequently for its improbability, its lack of narrative, its absence of dramatic tension, criticized, in short, for being what the formalists would have called 'unmotivated'.

But if the Jacobean texts continually remark beneath their breath or in loud clear voices, 'Regard me: I am a play', or if it was sometimes necessary for them, in order to achieve a sufficient extraordinariness, to double the stakes and let the play within the play raise the density of representation to the second power, they are not thus unacceptable to naturalizing criticism on aesthetic grounds alone, but because they share an unbroken continuity – across the proscenium *which is not there* – with the world in which they were performed, and which they perform. It is difficult, perhaps impossible, now to imagine a settlement in which the means of representation are so clearly visible as such: an artisanal world in which the device is naked not out of polemical technique but as its normal condition; a discursive situation before production has quite 'disappeared' into, in one of its modalities, the closed factory, or at the level of representation, into the conventions of that bourgeois naturalism which has nothing to do with nature, and everything to do with naturalizing the suppression of the signs of the artefact's production. A world of other visibilities than our own, which is founded on *their* elision, and whose suppression the reception of the texts rehearses.

Brecht understood this when he turned back to this early stage for material for his own alienated political theatre. But if Brecht's project was, by the elaboration of that series of theatrical interventions now known by the portmanteau 'alienation effect', to distance and break the mystificatory illusion near the end of its reign, the Jacobean theatre was, so to speak, anti-naturalist before the event. If there are seeds of an incipient naturalism growing up within it, so are there instances of it struggling to contain and ward them off: if Hamlet called on discourse to hold a mirror up to nature, at least the mirror could be seen for what it was. And nowhere more so – in a fine example of the typical lying at what we had been told were the margins – than in a text that criticism has consigned to obscurity, but which was in its time the most notorious of political plays; suppressed by troops after an unprecedented nine consecutive performances but none the less containing the essential figure of this unacceptable visuality where representation is itself present to representation. In the second seduction scene of Thomas Middleton's *A Game at Chesse* (the 'characters' and the general figuration of the play are worked out within a flagrantly unnatural chess trope) the White Queen's Pawn is momentarily entrapped by the device of an Egyptian mirror. She has been told that it is an enchanted mirror which will show her the man she is to marry. She is the desired object of the Black Bishop's Pawn, a Jesuit, who has attempted her seduction once by giving her a tract on religious obedience and, after the chaste White Queen's Pawn has absorbed its lesson, exacting a kiss as an exercise in subordination to a spiritual superior. Now, in the second attempt, the Black Jesuit appears on stage behind the White Queen's Pawn disguised as a gallant 'in rich attire like an apparition'. She, catching sight of what she thinks is a magic and privileged perception but which, even in the reality of the play, is no more than a plain glass, is thus captivated by his image. In the scene immediately following the Jesuit encounters the Black Knight's Pawn, a castrator, who at once recognizes the still-disguised priest by deciphering the coded inscription on his hatband (undercover Jesuit missionaries used such devices for mutual recognition).

The spectacular layers of this scene are complex. The woman is not allowed to look on reality direct but must glimpse it in a mirror which offers extraordinary sight but which is in fact a plain source of danger. The reality is itself disguised. In contrast to the White Queen's Pawn's earlier act of inefficient reading by which she became ensnared in power and vulnerable to sexual assault by having interpreted written signs literally and naïvely, the Black Knight's Pawn is able to read successfully through the dissembled text. And the devices are laid bare as the play, in its radicalism, uncertainizes its own ideological categories by drawing attention to their constructedness by means of the arbitrary and unconcealed theatricality with which it must engineer the White, Protestant, English, virtuous Pawn's escape from Black, Catholic, Spanish perfidy. To do this it first uses the cover of an unmotivated 'noise within', and it then extricates her from threatening specular captation by the equally unmotivated eventuality of another, Black, character's stratagems, which are not intrinsically related to the matter in hand but which unconsciously give political viability to the 'wrong' side. But of overriding and exemplary importance for this theatre is the fact that the whole is itself surrounded by another set of lines of sight by which the audience views everything without illusion. It is always aware of the real nature of the dissimulated glass, the 'identity' behind the disguise, and the functional purpose of the episode as a whole, although these are hidden from the White Pawn. There *is* a visual obscurity here, but it is confined to the stage, and there, to the object pawn against whose body the seduction and the assault are directed. It is not a deep obscurity in the sense that the place from which the scene is viewed is either clouded or confused.

The decoding of this structure involves a significant account of the gendering of the instance of power, to which we shall return, linked to a historical transition from sight to script as the medium of political facility and encratic difficulty: that the efficient reader is also a male castrator no doubt recounts a corporeal history of its own. But above all it is necessary to see that the problematicity of the scene – its gender dominations and its ideological and, indeed, political transactions – are realized in the graphic stage devices which overwhelmingly mark the visual and the specular as the plane of this theatre's signification. Only beyond our own naturalism will it be possible fully to comprehend that the audience was never captivated by the illusion because the spectacle never produced itself as other than what it was. This is why it is right to speak of the Jacobean device as innocent (from a representational rather than from a moral or political point of view): the device did not need to be at a distance when its erasure had not yet been secured. A subsequent cultural and historical movement clawed representation back from these outer limits of visibility into the duller and more treacherous reaches where the signifier is effaced and the specific gravity of representation bled off in favour of the theoretically naïve but politically powerful regime of the simple transcription of nature itself. The bourgeoisie, forgetting its revolutionary past as quickly as was decently possible (and, in England at least, before the classes beneath could learn anything of significance from it), soon constructs its own discursivity within which it is next to impossible to think the proposition that the represented – historical reality itself – is a thing produced, and not as in Pepys, voyeuristically and largely passively contemplated. It remains a pressing contemporary task to continue Brecht's work and in transvaluating the reception of the pre-naturalist Jacobean theatre to mobilize it as a critical weapon against the very naturalism that stifled it: not complacently to elide its difference, but to redeem, in a sense which Benjamin would have understood, that alterity.

But the reception of the Jacobean text-world we have been discussing does not reject solely these formal properties of that discursivity. It is their inextricable conjunction with the corporeality of the early seventeenth-century world that fully explains their denial by criticism anxious to disavow a materiality on whose de-realization its tradition is founded. Almost without exception, the depravity of the tragic dramatist who resorts to sensation is most clearly in evidence, it is said, in the presentation on stage of the body and the violence done to it. But is it utterly accidental, or even simply Webster's doubtful opportunism, that in the waxworks scene in *The Duchess of Malfi* it is the *corpses* of Antonio and the children that are displayed; or that in the same series of torments, at the far limits of theatrical pathos, the masque of the lunatics, doubling the spectacle within the spectacle, is in such close proximity to the episode of the severed hand? Is there not, perhaps, a more internally robust connection between the dramatic scene and the seen body

21

than one merely of perversity of taste when Macbeth's head is brought in, or Annabella's bleeding heart on the point of a dagger? Or when the body of Sejanus, like that of Cinna the poet before him, is torn in pieces at a moment of politics in a mass form? It is, of course, possible that merely a certain delicacy of touch in respect of corporeal pain, an artistry which we have lost, smears the poison of Vindice's revenge on the lipless skull of his raped and murdered mistress, from where, transmitted by a half-dead kiss, it eats away first the mouth and then the brain of the old Duke, while Hippolito holds down the man's dying tongue with the point of his knife. Or perhaps just a reflection of the available technology? But it would be better, more historically sensitive, to ask what inner cast of sociality governs the putting out of Gloucester's eyes and the corporeal extravagance of the now significantly seldom performed *Titus Andronicus*. For despite the fact that our own world has its share of torturers, a mark of difference from ourselves can be read in these and the other versions of the spectacular body with which the Jacobean stage is redolent. Especially when beyond that missing proscenium, in 'reality' itself, lies the mutilation that Prynne suffered for his discursive offences, or the public death which was exacted on another stage (Marvell does not fail to grasp the essential connection in his 'An Horatian ode') of the king himself. These images of the body are not instances of the arbitrary perversity of single dramatists, nor even the casual brutalities hidden away in underground cells or distant camps by violent but irredeemably furtive governments, but the insistence in the spectacle of a corporeality which is quite other than our own. The visibility of this body in pain – the pre-disciplinary body extant before that incarceration which is disclosed, in their different ways, both by Foucault's work and by the Pepysian text – is systemic rather than personal; not the issue of an aberrant exhibitionism, but formed across the whole surface of the social as the locus of the desire, the revenge, the power and the misery of this world.

The spectacular body in whose language Lady Macbeth must define her conditions and demands, and against whose measure Hamlet's anachronistic inwardness will have to be assessed, is everywhere present as the object and site of the confrontations which articulate the drama of this settlement. Continually evoked and displayed, close to language itself, the impersonal body is almost promiscuous in the repeated urgency with which it installs itself in the metaphors and concepts of this world, as well as in its practical situations. But properly it can only be regarded in this way because a certain emphasis is polemically necessary against the decentration it later suffers in history and in historiography alike. 'That a king may go a progress through the guts of a beggar' (*Hamlet*, IV. iii. 29-30) is extraordinary (if it is so at all) for its insistence on the democracy of mortality in contrast with the hierarchized body politic of the living world, not for the corporeal expression in which the idea emerges. The proliferation in the dramatic, philosophical and political texts of the period of corporeal images which have become dead metaphors for us – by a structured forgetting rather than by innocent historical wastage – are the indices of a social order in which the body has a central and irreducible place. Whether judicially tortured as the visible sign of the vengeance of the king on the transgressor, or disassembled lovingly on stage in the cause of poetry, it is the crucial fulcrum and crossing point of the lines of force, discursive and physical, which form this world as the place of danger and aspiration to which the Jacobean texts repeatedly attest. The glorious cruelties of the Jacobean theatre thus articulate a mode of corporeality which is structural to its world. Although the involvement of the body in punishment is only an essential and typical section across the way in which discourse invests it with a fundamental (and therefore, in this world, *superficial*) meaning, it none the less represents a generalized condition under which the body, living or dead, is not that effaced residue which it is to become, beneath or behind the proper realm of discourse, but a materiality that is fully and unashamedly involved in the processes of domination and resistance which are the inner substance of social life. The stage of representation and that other scaffold of corporal punishment are, as Marvell saw, effectively continuous with each other. On both, the spectacularly visible body is fully in place within signification, coterminous with the plane of representation itself. Unlike the secret half-life to which the Pepysian corporeality has been assigned, but from which it continues nevertheless to agitate the newly sovereign speech of a disembodied and Cartesian subjectivity, this early body lies athwart that divide between subject and object, discourse and world, that characterizes the later dispensation. The body of the world and that of the text are frequently identified with each other in the ideology of the Renaissance, but the metaphor should be understood with a nominalism appropriate to a period that antedates the deleterious separations on which modernity is founded. At the signifying centre of the culture they are at one with each other in the figure of the Passion, where the word and the body are inextricably identified in an act of punishment and signification from which all other meanings flow: the spirit who is the one real Subject of this world is wholly immanent, incarnate, in the flesh. The Jacobean body is at once sacred and profane, tortured and celebrated in the same gesture, because it traverses even the polarities of the culture's investments: or rather, it is the medium and the substance in which, ultimately, those meanings are inscribed. It has this polyvalent but unambiguous status because drawn on its surface are the means by which the culture, even at its most metaphysical, can determine not only its consonances but its inner discords as well. The underpinnings of the more quotidian disputes which texture the life of this society return in their grounding to that unseparated word made flesh which is the principle of its representational practices (practices which cannot, thus, be regarded as *representational* in the strictest sense). A mode of discourse operates here which, basing itself in incarnation, exercises a unitary *presence* of meaning of which the spectacular body is both the symbol and the instance.

That the body we see is so frequently presented in fragments, or in the process of its effective dismemberment, no doubt indicates that contradiction is already growing up

24

within this system of presence, and that the deadly subjectivity of the modern is already beginning to emerge and to round vindictively on the most prevalent emblem of the discursive order it supersedes. But despite the violence unleashed against the body, it has not yet been quenched. However much it has been subsequently ignored, it remains in the texts themselves as a vital, full materiality. The Jacobean body – the object, certainly, of terrible pressures – is distributed irreducibly throughout a theatre whose political and cultural centrality can only be measured against the marginality of the theatre today; and beyond the theatre it exists in a world whose most subtle inner organization is so different from that of our own not least because of the part played by this body in it. In the fullest sense which it is now possible to conceive, from the other side of our own carnal guilt, it is a *corporeal* body, which, if it is already touched by the metaphysic of its later erasure, still contains a charge which, set off by the violent hands laid on it, will illuminate the scene, incite difference, and ignite poetry. This spectacular visible body is the proper gauge of what the bourgeoisie has had to forget.

It is also therefore the body proper to that bright plenum which surrounds, but fails initially to include, Hamlet, whose world is laden, top-heavy with visibility: a world where everyone, in principle at least, assisted at the spectacle. In the crowded chamber soldiers lean on their halberds, perhaps half-listening, or just waiting for the changing of the guard. Knots of courtiers are gathered beneath the dais, absorbing the king's words: some, like Osric, fawning; others no doubt harbouring their own reservations about the legitimacy of the succession but, experienced in the naked, sudden and direct forms of power which mark their epoch, gravely keeping their own counsel. Servants move among the throng with sweet wine and honey cakes. Court officials are busy at a side-table near the throne. One cuts a quill with a small silver penknife, while another turns the ambassadors' letters patent in his delicate white fingers. Rumours of war stir and eddy there. The queen's face is expressionless, mask-like. A musician tunes a string in the alcove beside the great fireplace, crouched over his lute, one ankle resting on the other knee, the instrument cradled against his leg. Two hunting dogs lie sleepily on the rushes while the business of state murmurs around them. The sombre prince waits to one side.

There is apparently nothing here that cannot be seen. From the first apparition to that last procession when four sad captains carry the dead prince to the stage where his body will lie displayed *in state*, the moment of reality is the moment of sight. Elsinore is a place of spies and actors, actual and metaphorical, where scenes are played out to acknowledged and unacknowledged audiences, and where sight transfixes or is stolen, but is never doubted as the dominant mode of a (sometimes fraudulent) access.

The *teatrum mundi* has been taken as a metaphor, and this is today an intelligible mistake. But it is closer to a literalism in respect of this social plenum than a metaphor of contingent artifice. There is no well-founded division between those who perform and those who are spectators, between the subjects and objects of communicative sight: as one performs before another, she or he is at once regarded by a third, and so on throughout a network of asymmetrical observations patterning the entire space of being. It is not that there are no professional actors in this world (although they are of comparatively recent emergence, and their historical moment is properly yet to come), but that their condition repeats so closely – as the Jacobean texts continually insist – that of those others who are, of necessity here, but poor players of life itself. A condition, moreover, in which the *exteriority* of meaning is enacted in the foregrounding of the role and the part which the theatrical figuration of this world deploys. In *Hamlet*, social life is a succession of brightly lit tableaux set against black backgrounds whose darkness is not the symbol of a mysterious alterity, but simply the meaninglessness of the void beyond the surface of signification itself.

The spectacle is not without its ambiguities, however, for

in Denmark one may smile and smile and be a villain. Nor does the visual fullness of Hamlet's world entail the assumption of a plenitude of utter transparency: we must always beware the myth of better times that lies in wait for all our projections back beyond the modern. But it simply affirms that the dominant of this world, and of these texts, crossed and recrossed by dense lines of sight, is its spectacularity functioning as a concrete metaphor of presence; that even the error of this world is a riddle in its crowded visuality. So many of the notorious cruces for interpretative criticism and for the figures that populate this world turn upon ambiguous or deceitful appearance, that the commonplace name of seeming has been given to the problem. It is less frequently remarked that its system of signification is still secure enough, even as the crisis gathers in *Hamlet*, for false appearances only to be discernible as such against the surer measure of the true and the real, whether this be personified on stage in an omniscient dramaturge-seer, a Prospero, or vouchsafed to a knowing audience which accepts by convention that it can penetrate the disguise, while those within the action cannot. But in either case, and even if seeming is not the *profound* difficulty which criticism in its paucity has tried to make it, the arena of error and danger, of truth and its dissimulation, remains this complex of signs, devices and visualities.

Hamlet's world is riddled with difficulties: its alienation on the other side of naturalism, its own internal seeming, and, as we shall see, an incipient modernity. But in achieving its most explicit character in an interplay of visibilities, is this world not also one of relentless surfaces, without depth or mystery? This question formulates a crucial problem. For the moment it can be answered provisionally if enigmatically by remarking that it has only one modern depth because only one individual inhabits it, and even he is putative. For now it is enough to define the kind of obscurity, of difficulty, that is truly this world's and not his. Although the play, by turns ghostly and conspiratorial, is not lacking in the promise of mystery, it is of a very qualified kind, for all the conspiracies of the night are revealed, finally, and the whispered conversations overheard. There is little that remains ultimately opaque. Even Ophelia's madness moves in this world as the emblem of an indelible grief, but not as a diagnostic problem. Its typical figure is not Hamlet, but Polonius behind the arras. A thin veil hangs between him and the action that destroys him, a tapestry that conceals his presence but does not transform it. He learns nothing there. He dies because he is hidden, but his slaughter is one of the casual ones which Horatio survives to narrate in a place conservatively simplified again by Hamlet's *necessary* death. In no essential way do Polonius and his destiny encounter each other in the passage of the prince's blade through the fibres of the arras; his mistake, if such it is, is to be momentarily out of sight, not to be worthy or even desirous of such a death.

This world achieves its depth not in the figure of interiority by which the concealed inside is of another quality from what is external, but by a *doubling of the surface*. Just as *The Mousetrap* layers a spectacle within the spectacle, so the sheet of the action may be folded over until an unexpected contact is made and a sudden discharge of violence touched off. But the meaning of the action is generated in the productivity of the figures inscribed on the planer surfaces of the body of the text. *The Mousetrap* does not function to discover a truth (except in the most literal sense of discovery), for this is one of the few murder stories where the identity of the killer is revealed on the first page – and even if ghosts cannot be trusted, this operates as a vehicle of Hamlet's delay rather than as a real epistemological problem – but serves to organize in transit the necessary anxiety which must flow from and around the incestuous usurpation. It acts as a bridge between nodes of the extremely attenuated action (not much actually happens at Elsinore) rather than as an instrument of the revelation of a hidden mystery. This accounts for its curious, frustrated lack of consequence. Hamlet does not sweep to his revenge impelled by the proof of Claudius's guilt which the play within the play provides, because it isn't a *proof* of anything that was in doubt. *The Mousetrap* draws a line across the surface, an articulation in the diagram of the action. It functions to extend time rather than to excavate a hidden level of reality. Apart from the one great exception to the rule of this theatre's space, the reality of this world is utterly single, however it may be folded over on itself.

That Hamlet's first argument with his stepfather takes place in the crowded council chamber marks off this spectacular, corporeal sovereignty from the polity which is to succeed it. There is, however, no difficulty in recognizing, even from the present, the scene of the state. The language and the costume may not be that of our own day, but nor are we – on the surface – without sure points of reference here. Conducted under a different historical form, but clearly identifiable as such even from the contemporary standpoint of a very different experience of the political, central affairs of state are centrally enacted: the succession of rule, and the emergency of war. Claudius's opening disquisition on the haste with which his marriage to Gertrude has followed on the death of the former king her husband, by way of a nicely turned contrast between mourning and celebration, manages to sound at once sorrowing and festive. It is the accomplished palliative speech of an adept politician reassuring anxieties at home. He is convincing, genial, magnanimous, clearly adroit in managing councils of state. The next item of business touches foreign policy: Fortinbras has sharked up his list of lawless resolutes in the marches and now challenges for the control of disputed territory. Old rights are involved, not least the honour of the dead king, which Claudius does not fail to mention, skilfully linking the external threat to the internal problem, subtly buttressing his legitimacy by establishing himself as a defender of the memory of his predecessor against the foreign invader. War grows out of such things, and Denmark's armourers and shipwrights are already preparing for the conflict, but Claudius will pursue the options of diplomacy before unleashing the violence of this warlike state against the mercenaries. A certain political circumspection governs his instructions to the ambassadors who are fiercely ordered not to overstep the limits of their commission. In this, the primal scene of the play, the fully political concerns of the internal and external security of the realm itself are dramatized. Written at a moment in England's political history when both press heavily on the real kingdom, the scene delineates process of government with a clarity that is as economical as it is essential. The destiny of an entire society is gathered into these few lines and placed before audiences who will themselves participate at a drama of historical crisis. Denmark and England each stand on a threshold of change: by the end a certain greatness will have gone out of one; revolution will transform the other.

But there is an anachronistic temptation to read back from the present and identify, in the next business of the scene, as it shifts from the empowering of the ambassadors to the matter of Laertes's departure from court, with a *caesura* dividing off the political state from the more intimate textures of family life. Hardly high policy on a level with what has already been transacted in this busy hall, does this episode not serve to reformulate the scene, and to manage a transition from the public space to the personal and domestic argument with Hamlet that is to follow? To think so would be to commit a signal historical mistake. At most the items on this agenda are organized according to a descending order of importance, and even that is questionable in view of the subsequent unfolding of the action. The narrative of the drama (which should not, in any event, be confused with the form of the social situation it discloses) will foreground the particular trajectories of Hamlet substantially, and Laertes to an extent; but this must not be allowed to occlude its location of these destinies within the menace of the wider crisis, and more profoundly, within a density and order of being that defers the modern division.

In sharp contrast to the separations which the Pepysian text describes, in this polity, Laertes's departure is fully *in place* in the business of state. The king's permission – sued for in full council – doubles, complements, sanctions and

30

completes the reluctant permission of the biological father. The scene inscribes within itself not a separation of spheres but that relation of subordinate correspondence, theorized with varying degress of mysticism at the time, between the father who is as a king in the family and the king who is as a father in the state. Nor should this similitude be thought as pallid analogy or distant likeness. It is stricter than homology, and constitutes an essential link in a chain of ideal connections that ground sociality itself in a theory of kingship and kinship which was practised in an array of political, juridical and cultural institutions, and which articulates a social body that is layered, figured, but one. Organized under the general form of hierarchy, sanctioned in practice by force and metaphysically by God the King and God the Father whose just order it reflects, the single realm describes a full place, tense with patterns of fealty, reciprocity, obligation and command. The figure of the king guarantees, as locus and source of power and as master-signifier, a network of subsidiary relations which constitute the real practice and intelligibility of the lives of subjects.

If the body of the Passion is the foundation of this world's signifying, at the same time the body of the king is its coherent temporal instance, the body that encompasses all mundane bodies within its build. But the subjection at work here is not that modern form for which the ambitiously inappropriate name of 'consciousness' is frequently used. Pre-bourgeois subjection does not properly involve subjectivity at all, but a condition of dependent membership in which place and articulation are defined not by an interiorized self-recognition – complete or partial, percipient or unknowing, efficient or rebellious – (of none the less socially constituted subject-positions), but by incorporation in the body politic which is the king's body in its social form. With a clarity now hard to recapture, the social plenum *is* the body of the king, and membership of this anatomy is the deep structural form of all being in the secular realm. Where post-Pepysian subjection will distance the external world in order to construct subjectivity as the (imaginary) property of inner selfhood, this sovereignty achieves its domination

31

by other means, across an articulated but single ground. It establishes a constitution within which subjects are profoundly implicated not because they 'know their place' (as in the modern form when it is effective) but because alterity of placement is always-already encoded as unthinkable. Or at least no more conceivable than the absurd proposition that the arm could take the place of the spleen. This did not prevent rebellion, but the heavy price legitimacy extracts for such an act is the burden of dismembering the frame of place and sense itself.

In this scene, in *Hamlet*, the king and the biological father happen to be different people. But not far away in the *oeuvre*, in a significantly more conservative text, they are identical. When Lear sets his tragic action in motion by dividing the indivisible kingdom, there are a number of different registers to his error (one of the glories of the Renaissance is the pre-Rationalist *complexity* of its error). The historical register involves regression across a century of painful development. Under the Tudor dynasty England had emerged from internal wars to lay the groundwork of a nation state. The Crown, in breaking the authority of the feudal magnates and in rearticulating under its own sovereignty that of the Church, acquired the national monopoly of the means of both persuasion and violence. By skilful manipulation of class and factional alliances both with and over the heads of the lords ecclesiastical and temporal, it reorganized the power previously vested in them. The imposition of a professional central bureaucracy, and of local administrative and judicial government staffed increasingly by royal appointees, appeared to disseminate control at the same time as it effectively gathered it to the writ of the Crown. But Lear, in his *historical* folly, refragments the realm by dividing it among his daughters and re-establishing, under a nominal and ineffectual monarch, powerful and competitive baronial factions, whose gender only serves to underline their monstrous character.

If today an effort of retrospective imagination is needed in order to perceive the catastrophic enormity of this, to contemporaries its implications were plain and fearsome.

And not simply because of the threat posed by this dismemberment of the integrity of the realm. For in another register, but at the identical moment and not as a consequential effect, Lear's action – which is already close to that madness that will soon bear down on him – also disarticulates the order of the family. If Hamlet's first argument with Claudius takes place in state, in the first scene of *Lear* the fusion (of what is in any case not yet separate) is also total. Even without that signal blindness which permeates the play as a terrible instance of debility in the spectacular kingdom and whose first act is to misrecognize Cordelia and cast her, rather than her sisters, in the role of rebellious daughter-subject, the king's original intention of a tripartite division of the realm and the family violates an essential coherence between them both. Its intention threatens to disassemble authority relations fundamental to this patriarchal sovereignty, and to the very code of being it describes. Lear cannot abdicate his position, in family or state, as if it were the public office of a later polity. In this settlement, soon to be unsettled and surrendered to lawlessness because the place of the king-father from which the law is uttered is soon to be emptied, subjects are located in places not by the *apparently* auxiliary contingency of the later constitution, but by an essential fit, by necessary bonds of nature articulating the political anatomy of the king's body. Although disorder in the family, in the state and in the faculties of the soul – and, indeed, in cosmic nature – can act as metaphors for each other, their substantial interrelation is more profound than poetic artifice: they are all grounded at once in the same inner correspondence whose transgression risks the disarticulation of reality itself. It is with the *same* gesture of division that Lear fissures his kingdom, his family and his reason, for on this scene the state, kinship and sense repeat and extend into each other without break.

Thus Laertes's suit for permission to travel and the fourth item on the agenda which is much more problematic from the standpoint of the present – Hamlet's melancholic excess of mourning, and the Oedipal drama that begins to speak itself there – are heard in the crowded council chamber.

What would appear under the new regime as private matters exist in an as yet undivided continuum with the succession and the gathering war. The public and the private as strong, mutually defining, mutually exclusive categories, each describing separate terrains with distinct contents, practices and discourses, are not yet extant. In *Hamlet* and in *Lear*, and in the wider sovereignty they disclose, the space of being, the society, the world – what you will – is ordered along different lines from those that fissure our own situation. This is not to insist that there is no aloneness there. Ophelia's lonely epithet for Hamlet himself – 'The glass of fashion and the mould of form,/The observ'd of all observers' (IV.i. 156-7) – certainly marks out around the prince, in significantly specular language, a penumbra of solitude. But this is not a private condition. The keynote is the very visibility with which the space is delineated: it is the pertinent metaphor, as concrete as any could be, for the indivisibility of the plenum. The sovereignty that governs this space – however insecure it is growing as it registers in the resort to the figure of the spy, or in Lear's and Gloucester's blindness, its progressive *failure to see* – is represented by the all-pervading access which the spectacle provides. This is why so many stand around, paying attention or not, near the action at the throne, in the centre of the kingdom and of the family. They and we are attentive or indifferent, but *necessary* spectators here, not because the action only acquires its meaning when it is apprehended by an audience for whom it is played out, but because no other conditions are extant. In the same way as what is seen does not take place in public, so what is not seen by all does not work itself out in private. What is secret in this world – the conspiracies of the night, two figures who stand together on an empty beach – does not correspond to that modern condition of privacy in which the Pepysian subject is incarcerated. Here even solitude, while it may be a form of torture, is a figure of the whole, contingent on the local and momentary situation, but not a rent in the social fabric as such.

And yet, to return to the great hall, which has been named with an aptness that is uncanny the *presence* chamber (for everything in this sovereignty is exactingly present, sanctioned by the real or in principle proximity of the body of the king), we must take the measure of the one great exception to the rule of this world: beside the throne, slightly apart from the others, his head bowed in thought, stands the Oedipal prince. In what are almost the first words we hear him speak, a claim is made for modern depth, for qualitative distinction from the corporeal order of the spectacle:

> Seems, madam! nay it is, I know not 'seems'.
> 'Tis not alone my inky cloak, good mother,
> Nor customary suits of solemn black,
> Nor windy suspiration of forced breath,
> No, nor the fruitful river in the eye,
> Nor the dejected haviour of the visage,
> Together with all forms, modes, shapes of grief,
> That can denote me truly. These indeed seem,
> For they are actions that a man might play,
> But I have that within that passes show,
> These but the trappings and the suits of woe.
>
> (I.ii. 75-86)

Hamlet asserts against the devices of the world an essential interiority. If the 'forms, modes, shapes' fail to denote him truly it is because in him a separation has already opened up between the inner reality of the subject, living itself, as 'that within that passes show', and an inauthentic exterior: and in that opening there begins to insist, however prematurely, the figure that is to dominate and organize bourgeois culture. Seen from the viewpoint of this speech, the narrative of *Hamlet* is nothing but the prince's evasion of a series of positionalities offered to him by the social setting. From the moment when the ghost of his father lays on him the burden of vengeance, his passage through the drama is the refusal of – or, at most, the parodic and uncommitted participation in – the roles of courtier, lover, son, politician, swordsman, and so on. Even the central task of revenge provides, in its deferral, no more than a major axis of the play's duration. But in dismissing these modes, or 'actions'

35

as he calls them, Hamlet utters, against the substance of the spectacular plenum which is now reduced in his eyes to a factitious artificiality 'that a man might play', a first demand for the modern subject. In the name, now, not of the reign of the body but of the secular soul, an interior subjectivity begins to speak here – an I which, if it encounters the world in anything more than a quizzical and contemplative manner, must alienate itself into an environment which inevitably traduces the richness of the subject by its mute and resistant externality. An early embarrassment for bourgeois ideology, and one of which Hamlet is in part an early victim, was that even as it had to legitimize the active appropriation of the world, it also had to encode its subject as an individual, privatized and largely passive 'consciousness' systematically detached from a world which is thus beyond its grasp: for all its insistence on the world as tractable raw object it none the less constructs a subjectivity whose form is that of the unique and intransitive soul, centred in meanings which are apparently its alone.

But this interiority remains, in *Hamlet*, gestural. 'The heart of my mystery' (III. ii. 368-9), as he describes it to Guildenstern in another place, is the real opacity of the text. Unlike those other obscurities of seeming which are *proper* to the spectacle, the truth and density of *this* mystery can never be apprehended. The deceptions of the plenum which surrounds Hamlet are always ultimately identifiable as such, and therefore only obscure for a few or within some tactical situation of the drama as it unfolds: they are never beyond the reach of its epistemology. But Hamlet's inner mystery is not of this order. Neither those who seek it out within the play, who try to discover whether he is mad in reality or 'in craft', nor the audience who overhear so many examples of the rhetorical form proper to this isolated subjectivity, the soliloquy, are ever placed by the text in a position from which it can be grasped. It perdures as a central obscurity which cannot be dramatized. The historical prematurity of this subjectivity places it outside the limits of the text-world in which it is as yet emergent only in a promissory form. The text continually offers to fulfil the claim of that first speech, but whenever it appears that the claimed core of that within which passes the show of the spectacle will be substantially articulated, Hamlet's riddling, antic language shifts its ground and the text slides away from essence into a further deferral of the mystery. But if the text cannot dramatize this subjectivity, it can at least display its impossibility, when Hamlet offers a metaphor of himself, of his self, to Guildenstern who is an instrument, purely, of the king, and signally lacking any form of interiority. Challenging Guildenstern to 'pluck out the heart' of his mystery – in language sufficiently corporeal to point the failure – Hamlet gives him the recorder which he cannot play, although he would, in Hamlet's conceit, 'sound' the 'compass' of the prince. The hollow pipe is the refutation of the metaphysic of soul which the play signals but cannot realize. For Hamlet, in a sense doubtless unknown to him, is truly this hollow reed which will 'discourse most eloquent music' but is none the less vacuous for that. At the centre of Hamlet, in the interior of his mystery, there is, in short, nothing. The promised essence remains beyond the scope of the text's signification: or rather, signals the limit of the signification of this world by marking out the site of an absence it cannot fill. It gestures towards a place for subjectivity, but both are anachronistic and belong to a historical order whose outline has so far only been sketched out.

It is into this breach in Hamlet that successive generations of criticism – especially Romantic and post-Romantic variants – have stepped in order to fill the vacuum and, in explaining Hamlet, to explain him away. This effort to dissipate the challenge he represents is partly explained by the need to remake the Jacobean settlement in the eternal image of the bourgeois world, and partly by a more subversive potential in the prince. Accounts of his unresolved Oedipus complex, his paranoia – both clinical and vulgar – his melancholic nobility of soul in a world made petty by politics have all served the purposes of bourgeois criticism's self-recognition. In erasing the alterity of this other world it has sought to discover there the same preoccupations and structures as those which govern its own discourse. Politically liberal versions of this unconscious and ideologically loaded modernization of the pre-revolutionary sovereignty, articulating what is either a mild criticism or simply the inheritance of a soured Cartesianism, have even discovered in the prince – fully fledged – that alienated modern individual dejected in the market-place of inauthentic values. Each has found it necessary to discover in him one recension or another of the subjectivity which defines the modern soul. But in so doing they have necessarily overstated the fullness of the consciousness actually dramatized by the text. The lack of closure in its relentless scepticism, its relativizing, unstable discourse, have been blocked and frozen in order to provide the fixity necessary to recuperate it to a conception of essential subjectivity *fully realized*. In place of the text's pattern of offer and refusal of this interiority, strung out along the chain of Hamlet's rich but fleeting language, a single 'problem', or knot of problems, is diagnosed, and is then said to denote him truly. The startling effect has been to reproduce the text as the great tragedy of . . . *bourgeois* culture.

But the point is not to supply this absence, to make whole what is lacking, but to aggravate its historical significance. *Hamlet* is a contradictory, transitional text, and one not yet fully assimilated into the discursive order which has claimed it: the promise of essential subjectivity remains unfulfilled. From its point of vantage on the threshold of the modern but not yet within it, the text scandalously reveals the emptiness at the heart of that bourgeois trope. Rather than the plenitude of an individual presence, the text dramatizes its impossibility. Not only is the myth by which the autonomous individual is made the undetermined unit of being, in contrast to an inert social world, alien to this dramatic regime, but even when, in a later settlement, the philosophical legislation and discursive underpinning necessary to support the device have been provided, it will achieve a success whose stability, as the example of Pepys shows, is at best fragile. When it does emerge in the discourse of a Descartes or a Pepys, in a different kind of writing from that of the Jacobean spectacle as its substantial and founding mode, it will immediately begin to be naturalized as the figure under which the social conditions of another sovereignty will be lived. Itself socially constructed none the less, and not in any event identical with those, or any, social conditions themselves – for in dividing the subject from the outer world it enacts an imaginary desocialization of subjectivity – it will take up its place as the central figure in which bourgeois society will be experienced in interiority and subjection. Its dramatic impossibility in *Hamlet* is, therefore, the more critically valuable for those like ourselves who must still live it out. Rather than a gap to be filled, the vacuity in Hamlet is a 'failure' to be celebrated against the more systematically vacuous dominion of the order of subjectivity it both signals and resists.

But if Hamlet's promised but unfulfilled interiority in its sharpest form is unacceptable to bourgeois ideology because it is not sufficiently fixated, it is equally intolerable to the plenum which surrounds him because it has already moved too far in that direction. The text, too, effects its own closure of the fissure that the prince opens in its fabric, and averts the challenge to its order which the prince represents. This is why it mobilizes so many simulacra of him. Fortinbras, Laertes, even the semi-mythical Pyrrhus of the First Player's speech – whose sword also hesitates above the head of a king – are each interference repetitions of Hamlet by which the text disperses across its surface (in a distribution fitted to the spatial dimension of the spectacle) other, external versions of the prince, in order to fend off the insistence of his unique essentiality. And it is why, in order that the play may end, a second Hamlet must be introduced. For rather than the maturation or development of 'character' that we have been taught to look for in Shakespeare, there is a quasi-Brechtian discretion between the figure who is deported to England and the figure who returns having suffered a sea-change. The agnostic melancholic is replaced by the man of action who does battle with the pirates, and who devises an effective stratagem against the king's agents which he sardonically reports to Horatio: 'So Guildenstern and Rosencrantz go to't' 'Why, man, they did make love to this employment'

39

(V.ii. 56-7). The Hamlet who delays (and whose delaying is but the linear deployment of the 'vertical' absence within) is replaced by one who simply waits, for whom 'it will be short, the interim is mine' (V.ii. 74): and who is soon dead; by one whose first appearance, at Ophelia's graveside, is signalled by the fact that the riddling, sliding language of the first Hamlet has now migrated to the mouth of the gravedigger from whom, ironically, the second must now try to elicit simple answers to simple questions; and, finally, by one who goes to his death inserted into the traditional Christian values – the 'special providence in the fall of a sparrow' (V.ii. 217-18) and the 'divinity that shapes our ends,/Rough-hew them how we will'(V.ii. 10-11) – that were so profoundly questioned by the figure he supplants. By these devices, arbitrarily and theatrically secured, the challenge of Hamlet's incipient modernity is extinguished – for a time – and the prince recuperated to the order of the spectacle which his opacity had troubled.

Tragic heroes have to die because in the spectacular kingdom death is in the body. There is no 'merely' or metaphorically ethical death which does not at the same time entail the extinction of the body, and even its complete and austere destruction. That pleasure will have to wait until the modern soul has taken its place within transformed discursive relations, at the centre of the stage of writing.

If we have identified in *Hamlet* a *historical* register of modernity, the Oedipal prince is, as they say, ahead of his time, when he calls on the 'too too solid flesh to melt' (I.ii. 129). His desire to refine away the insistent materiality of the body is the necessary complement to that interiority of soul which would otherwise realize itself utterly in him. As some criticism today – often with an equally ambivalent political valency – is attempting the radical deconstruction of the ground of our signification, so Hamlet admonishes the foundation of his dominant contemporary possibility for meaning. But the intense corporeality of the Jacobean spectacle that surrounds him and his dark, vacant mystery rejects him like an alien virus. The text-world rounds on him and is not content, finished, until by means it can only half-acknowledge it has reduced him to its own dimension. As the visible body which Fortinbras orders the four captains to carry 'to the stage' the unproductive prince is finally at one with the order of the plenum: or, in its master-language, 'most royal' (V.ii. 394-6).

But this triumph – and this reduction – does not elegiacally affirm that settlements prior to the exigencies of our own were without their rigours and contradictions. Nor even that they were particularly settled, as if the spectacular plenum were unchallenged (we have seen that it is not) or its forces perfectly balanced, unnaturalized because irresistible. Desire which is the motor is forever restless. A struggle is being fought out in these texts, and this is the lot of discourse, and of social life, in any polity organized under forms of domination. If the once-full body is so often presented as a shattered wreckage of disarticulated fragments, it is because the disintegration of this world and its signification is already upon it. As modern subjectivity begins to emerge, it turns destructively on that older body from which it struggles to free itself. If the anachronistic paradox of *Hamlet*, the non-homogeneity of the historical time of the soul and that of the encompassing spectacle can be deciphered (and it is only paradoxical when judged against a measure of textual unity and historical monism which should be, by now, antique), it is because the Jacobean scene, for all its dominant attachment to the old kingdom, is already touched by the marks of the gathering modern crisis on whose threshold this text-world stands.

*   *   *   *

And as for regulating the Presse, let no man think to have the honour of advising ye better than your selves have done in that Order publisht next before this, that no book be Printed, unlesse the Printers and the Authors name, or at least the Printers be register'd. Those which otherwise come forth, if they be found mischievous and libellous, the fire and the

41

> *executioner will be the timeliest and the most effectual remedy, that mans prevention can use.* (*Areopagitica*, p.353).

It is certainly an index of the depth of the crisis that these words, apart from a few lines serving as an *envoi*, conclude what is otherwise regarded as one of the great texts written against censorship. But that a writing which sets itself that task should end by handing discourse over to the executioner is only fully a paradox when viewed from the idealist standpoint of a plenitude of human speech. It is skewed when seen from the perspective of the principle of rarefaction which governs the actual distribution of human discourse. A full speech stands above its conditions, sufficient to itself, at once adequately grounded in its own meanings and at the same time aspiring to, if not already extant in, a universal and sacred realm of independent and discrete truths. But the discursive position which wishes to escape the antinomies (purely internal to a certain historicism) between the universal and the historical will have to recognize that even where discourse is globally implicative it is none the less locally relational, hollowed by the *strategic* character of its deployment. For this reason to contemplate *Areopagitica* as a significant document of some 'human freedom' would only be to assuage a particular restlessness in respect of the truth, and then only momentarily. To the extent that it has been thought in the past that Milton conceived of liberty and censorship as antitheses, it is now necessary to take his text's will to freedom at a little less than its face value, and to exercise a critical decoding rather than the more familiar appreciative summary. Discursively, *Areopagitica* operates to call into being a new state-form, and to inscribe there a novel citizen-subject. And it does this despite its argument. This is not to say that its substance is beside the point; on the contrary, censorship was a decisive experience of the seventeenth century, which has even managed to cover its own traces and disappear from the standard histories of the literature of the period which are silent on the subject; none the less,

Areopagitica is a document which arranged its arguments, its rhetoric and its metaphors – its utterance – among and across relations which it inscribes within itself without ever making them the evident object of its arguments or the manifest content of its speech. To say that these distinctions operate behind the back of the text, or as its unconscious, would be to risk too far the temptations of a metaphysic of depth which we have been at pains to avoid so far, despite the fact that it is the history of its emergence which we are tracing here. But the transactions of the text, in the *discursive* register, are in a real sense unknown to the text itself. In this sense it is similar in status to other fabular seventeenth-century script we are concerned to read here: not exhaustive; not permitting everything to be said about the new emergency; exemplary but not illustrative, a site of real inscription of the new relations and terms.

While an anecdote (although in no way trivial for being such) will not by itself deprive *Areopagitica* of its 'literary' truth and return it to its discourse, it will serve to indicate a pathway to the issue: Milton was never opposed to censorship, in fact we know that in 1651 he served as a licenser of news books, a state censor. If this only signals, as many have argued, that Milton was prepared to make a division in the field of discourse between those daily words too promiscuous not to come under the scrutiny of the governing authority and the graver products of 'the industry of a life wholly dedicated to studious labours' (296) (and thus, no doubt, more docile), this is at least to have dislodged his pamphlet from its universality. This relocation can be further effected by replacing the text within the preceding development of the means of policing discourse which the office of state for which he worked inherited. From the early part of the previous century through to what was to be one of the last executive acts of the Caroline government, the authorities established, elaborated and consolidated increasingly fierce and attentive measures to bring the printing and distribution of books under their direct or delegated control. The detail of this history is accessible elsewhere, but here some description of its main tendency will serve to point out the structural contrast between Milton's text and the developments anterior to it. Whichever aspect of the mechanism of control we examine, whether it be the trade-off by which the Crown granted the Stationers' Company a virtual monopoly on printing in return for the acceptance of overt or implicit responsibility for regulating the issue of its presses, or the more formal provisions for pre-publication licensing by officers of Church and state, in either case the period saw a strengthening and increasing sophistication of the censoring machine. From the Elizabethan Injunctions of 1559 to the Star Chamber decree of 11 January 1637 which provided for a largely professional censorship dealing with printed matter under separate expert categories, procedures were built up to ensure an ever more vigilant and pervasive control: the scope of materials coming within their purview was progressively widened, as were the means of enforcement, until the censorship, in these corporal times, had at its disposal an almost unlimited power to punish. By the time that the Long Parliament abolished Star Chamber and the other prerogative courts, a high wall of prohibition, surveillance and punishment had been built up around the printed word in whose supervision the government was prepared to invest enormous quantities of time, labour and expertise.

It would be wrong, however, to conclude that with the accession of Parliamentary forces this machinery was dismantled. For a period after the abolition of the Caroline executive courts there was a brief and unprecedented freedom of the press in which printing shops and their products proliferated. But within a few years, shaken by the explosion of written discourse which attended the breakdown of censorship, the same Parliament was soon enacting its own regulatory measures, including the Order of 14 June 1643, against which Milton wrote *Areopagitica*. The reanimated censoring machine – which met with widespread and sometimes armed popular resistance – was, in its essential outline, identical with the Star Chamber provisions. Although the personnel was changed and Parliamentary appointees substituted for the clerics and other delegates of the Caroline government, and the prerogative Crown authority to license was not re-established, the machinery itself was refined still further. Now nine categories of books were designated, and an even more precisely organized battery of licensers established to deal with them.

A small but decisive incision in this structure, and in the plenum of the old kingdom, is offered by *Areopagitica*. A feature common to all the preceding measures, whatever the degree of complexity of the censoring apparatus or the poignancy of its disposable violence, but which separates Milton's text from them, is that they each place the moment of state intervention before that of publication. *Areopagitica*, though also a call for censorship (slightly reduced in scope), places that moment in the production and distribution of discourse *after* it has 'come forth'. The pre-publication licensing of the Tudor, Stuart and early Parliamentary measures are those of a pre-emptive state designing to stop the publication of what were called, in a phrase surviving from the reign of Henry VIII, 'naughty books'; its powers were vengeful ones which bore down on the transgressions it had itself failed to prevent. The powers of the Miltonic 'provisions', however, are essentially deterrent (although also punitive). They offer to the discoursing subject the image of an eventuality of punishment which will occur if the offending book comes out, while she or he remains 'free' to publish it. This crucial difference between the Miltonic text and the history of censorship which goes before it (and, indeed, after it, for *Areopagitica*'s proposals were not enacted immediately) encodes two distinctly separate versions of the state and its relation to social life. The pre-Miltonic state acknowledges its existence as state, but one could say, without investing the state with a spurious benevolence, that it also assumes an essential continuity between itself and the subjects it incorporates. As we have remarked in *Lear* and *Hamlet*, the body of the king, the place of representation, and the correspondences of kinship, power and sense, are coterminous. This state knows no limits because in theory nothing is outside its domain. It is permissive only in the ungenerous sense that it seeks positively to supervise the production and the contents of discourse. Its paternalism is given in the fact that it assumes the father's role of a real and metaphysical authority which is all-pervasive, backed up by the angry recompense of punishment. But in the Miltonic 'state' – that set of relations marked out in *Areopagitica* – it is already possible to detect the outline of that modern settlement which founds itself on a separation of realms between the public arena of the state apparatus and another domain of civil life. Here a new liberty is encoded, although it is but a negative one. The subject, now emerging as a private citizen although not legally named as such in a constitution which is, to this day, unwritten, or – rather – 'inscribed elsewhere', may do as it pleases up to the point of transgression where its activity will be arrested by the agents of the apparatus who patrol the frontier between the two spaces.

But lest it be thought that this is simply a step along an even and uncomplex path from the old tyranny to a new and modern freedom, it is important to emphasize the extent to which what is proposed in *Areopagitica* represents a fresh form of control. What is to become the meagre political insubordination of a classical liberalism can be discerned even at this stage when Milton's text defines liberty as what is in any case the basis of its own political practice: not the positive freedom of a just order, but the *ex post facto* redress of grievances. And as he says, the attack on licensing is not intended to introduce licence. On the contrary all of Milton's descriptions of social life emphasize the stability, maturity and sobriety of the English nation. Far from the 'untaught and irreligious gadding rout' (336) which a preemptive censorship must assume the people to be, they are in fact characterized by a remarkable degree of that *self-discipline* which, along with other qualities associated with it, is to become the linchpin of a move articulated by the text from the unmediated and overt violence of the older settlement to a more indirectly ideological control implanted in the new subjectivity. The text defines the principal problem for government, the 'great art', as discerning 'in what the law is to bid restraint and punishment, and in what things perswasion only is to work' (318-19), and in a similar way, to censure the population 'for a giddy, vitious and ungrounded people' would be 'to the disrepute of our Ministers' whose 'exhortations, and the benefiting of their hearers' are to be among the central means of securing the required tranquility in what would otherwise be 'an unprincipl'd, unedify'd, and laick rabble' (328-9). The decisive moment of control is now to be not so clearly the sanction of punishment, as the inner discipline, the unwritten law, of the new subjection: for 'under pittance, and prescription, and compulsion, what were vertue but a name, what praise could be then due to well-doing, what grammercy to be sober, just or continent?' (319). The state succeeds in penetrating to the very heart of the subject, or more accurately, in pre-constituting that subject as one which is already internally disciplined, censored, and thus an effective support of the emergent pattern of domination. As Milton reminds us again and again, the new subject becomes the location of the new drama of individual conscience which 'doth make cowards of us all', or, as Hamlet might have said had he reflected in a different language on his political situation, ascertains each of us severally in obedience to a sovereignty whose head we dare not thus cut off. Conscience, assisted by that private reason, deliberation and judgement with which *Areopagitica* invests the bourgeois citizen, enters in the text into an essentially single battle with temptation (amongst whose 'objects of lust' (319), as Pepys discovered, are certain books) and in doing so interiorizes conflicts and dynamics which are newly encoded as belonging to subjectivity rather than to the social exterior.

It would, then, be a misplaced reception of *Areopagitica*'s separation of the old kingdom that succumbed to a euphoria of early liberation remembered (although bourgeois culture's self-universalization doubtless accounts for the timelessness of the text's alleged pertinence). At stake in Milton's call for 'civil liberty' is a control which is in some ways more profound than when such legislated or unlegislated rights are missing. In the settlement which begins to impinge here, the state secures its overall penetration on the basis of an apparent withdrawal and limitation of its pertinent domain: Milton accepts that in the realm of discourse at least, atheism and blasphemy might continue to be the state's concern, but allots the rest to the individual subject who 'searches, meditats, is industrious, and likely consults and conferrs with his judicious friends' (324), in short, to civil society. But by demarcating the public space of the state's competence from the private realm of individual freedoms, it has secured its domination there too, by securing the recto of its public verso. This is why *Areopagitica* remains the text of a new power despite its agonistic rhetoric of liberty. In addition, it is important that the essence of this power lies as much in the line of division between the public and the private (on either side of which lie – at another level to that we have been discussing – philosophical subjectivity over against an object-world) as in the substantive contents of what lies to either side of it. It is not that in the establishment of a domain of public authority and another area of private freedom, domination has been confined to one, and liberation released into the other, but that the division itself is the very form of the new power, grounded as much in the apparent freedom of even the choices allowed by Milton's benign pluralism as in its more overt controls. It is counter-intuitive and defies every instinct of common sense to insist that the inception of specific and more or less well-defined freedoms – 'free consciences and Christian liberties' (341-2) – is the effect of a powerful new dominion; but, without impugning the sacrifices of the women and men who gave their lives for these freedoms, that is the outcome. In the division between the two spheres is encoded an essential settlement which allots civil liberty to the subject only on condition that it is indeed *civil*, with all the well-ordered Roman and juridical connotations which seventeenth-century classicism, to be reinforced in the eighteenth-century, could add to the ideological registers of that word. The horror with which

Milton contemplates the logical consequence of the principle of licensing books when he remarks that it would necessitate the extension of control to every area of social life, to all discourse and representation, all styles of dress, each country dance, every guitar in every bedroom (while it foreshadows the absolute *disciplinary* surveillance which will be consolidated later) is now counterposed to the intrinsic sobriety of the people which argues against the need for detailed state control. That sobriety – we have noticed Pepys' somewhat equivocal use of the same notion – is the condition, in the sense both of a central feature of, and a condition of granting, even the provisional civil liberty envisaged by the text.

A few moments with the *Diary* of Philip Henslowe show that despite the firm attachment of authors' names to Jacobean play-texts today, the actual construction of the works, in so far as it was a commercial enterprise carried out largely by jobbing writers whose remuneration for odd additional scenes, revision and initial composition is recorded in Henslowe's accounts of payment, it was also a collaborative process. The firmness of the attachment of any author's name to text, let alone that of a single author who becomes, thus, fully and singly, the subject of that text, had then by no means an equal fixity with that which has been constructed subsequently, often by dint of elaborate and frequently wasted canonical scholarship. In Milton's discourse on discourse, however, an important step in the establishment of that fixity, and that writing subjectivity, is taken. *Areopagitica* twice refers approvingly to the Order of Parliament passed immediately before the licensing provisions against which it argues, which provided for the registration on publication of the names of author and printer, and for the protection of copyright vested, for the first time in English law, in the author. Although measures fully resembling modern copyright were only enacted by the so-called Statute of Anne at the beginning of the eighteenth century, the Miltonic evocation of the early measures is of great ideological significance. *Areopagitica* marks a shift in representative and central discourse from the performed writing of the early seventeenth-century stage to the more evidently 'written' writing of the later period: a transition from collaboration (of composition and performance) to individual production, and from visuality to script. And in the new discursivity, in which the text is fully in place for the first time, an essential relation of the author to that text is a property relation. Of course, in order to preserve the idealism of *Areopagitica* it is necessary to construct an imaginary division within discourse (formally identical to that opening up between body and soul) so that Truth, which Milton goes out of his way to insist should not be 'monopoliz'd and traded in by tickets and statutes, and standards . . . like our broad cloaths and our wooll packs' (327), can be spoken of separately from the book-commodity which is thus left free, by rhetorical sleight of hand, to enter the market-place. At the same time as the discoursing subject is newly confirmed in the domain of private liberty, the material writing of discourse also enters the 'free' exchange of civil society. Truth, the conveniently ideal form, hovers, naturally, above it.

The marks of this economy of discourse are not, however, as emphatic in the text as those defining the conditions of that discoursing subject, who must now – in a phrase which would have been resonant for Pepys – 'in a private condition, write' (*Areopagitica*, 293). Whether it be 'him who from his private house wrote that discourse to the Parlament of *Athens*' (296), that 'privat man' (316) to whom Plato forbade poets to read before their verse had been scrutinized by authority, or simply the phrase which adequately positions the subject in relation to the objects and the destination of discourse – 'When a man writes *to* the world' (324) – in each case the discursive location is clearly enunciated, and in addition the judicious and rational discrimination, imputed to the new subject in general, is the more insistently emphasized when it is overtly the subject of writing (or of reading). In seeking to extract the discoursing subject from state control, 'leaving it to each ones conscience to read or to lay by' (302), the text ever more clearly hands the subject over to that deeper control which we have already evoked. In doing so it signals the more graphically the profound implication of seventeenth-century discourse in the machinery of censorship, and in particular the imbrication of the founding moment of bourgeois discursivity, articulated as a socially hegemonic form, with that machinery.

That censorship was a constitutive experience for the seventeenth century – and for ourselves – needs stressing in view of the deletion of the entire problem from the history of writing. But if it is hardly possible to overemphasize its importance for the texts of the period, this should not be taken to refer only to the gross instances (although they should be identified and understood) where the censor's pen has left gaps in the text, but also to the *fullness* of the period's discourse. It has taken a historian writing on literature to notice what literary criticism has been studiously blind to. Christopher Hill shows that by a certain moment an entire literary mode – pastoral – could function as a set of coded symbols by which political statements could be enunciated in a form that would allow them to evade the censorship: with sufficient care in the manipulation of the stock conventions it could always be claimed that the poem was only about nymphs and shepherds after all. And centuries later literary 'critics' would agree . . . . But this evasive coding is itself only a relatively simple and external instance of discourse being conditional on censorship not in its elisions but in its substantial articulation. In a still profounder sense, as the example of the Cartesian text will show, although it is already clear in Pepys, the very structure of *all* bourgeois enunciation is governed by its relation to censorship as a determinant condition.

If this subjectivity is sketched in the seventeenth century, although perhaps not fully and ultimately consolidated as a phenomenon then, it is of crucial importance that its discourse, and the discourses in which it emerges, are censored ones. It is an essential link between the inner being of the subject, that interiority which was beginning to open up in *Hamlet* but for which the pre-bourgeois polity had no role, and the outer dimension of the state. While censorship is a state function, an exterior apparatus of control, in so far as the domain it polices is the production, circulation and exchange of discourses, it is one that reaches into the subject itself. It thus has a double function here, at once representative and substantive: representative in as much as it stands cross-sectionally for a whole ensemble of other changes brought about by the long process of the bourgeois revolution in the relationship between state and civil society, state and citizen, and for the opening-up of that division, a caesura missing from the Jacobean spectacle, or if present, only so in promissory form; but substantive in as much as it is the articulating mode of the bourgeois subject in discourse. When Milton's persona replied peremptorily to an imagined opponent 'The State Sir . . . The State shall be my governours, but not my criticks' (326), he offered a more consequential hostage to historical fortune than he imagined.

*   *   *   *

The defining feature of the bourgeois discursive regime is the *in situ* control – direct, or now more prevalently implicative – of the newly interiorated subject. From the standpoint of the politics of representation, that soul is also the necessary vehicle of the naturalistic empiricism which, in one form or another, including some which are technically rationalist, is to dominate the epoch. The modern subject is constructed as the bearer of naturalism, the facticity of things and their weightless transcription in discourse, in the first instance by an obvious device. The subject is contrasted to an outer world which, although 'social', becomes for it a kind of nature; whether fixed and irredeemable, or governed by those natural laws from whose precise externality not even Marx was entirely willing to free his language. For the first time it is possible to speak with some certainty of society – the associative name we give to lived isolation – when it has been effectively desocialized, its humane production elided by the separation from it of the constitution of the human subject. But the gross distinction between the individual subject and the social object-nature (set among the constellation of other separations between public and private, body and soul, state and civil society, and so on) conceals a subtler division which is none the less of greater moment in organizing the new regime. Not only is it now possible and necessary to narrate the outer world from an inner place, by means of a clarified and transparent instrumental language, and similarly to reflect on others as Other, but – more insidiously – the subject can, and now must, reflect on itself in the same fashion.

Descartes played the major part in providing the agonistic legitimation of this departure, in texts which are normally thought of as philosophical but which are at least as important for what they do as for what they say; in for example this famous passage from the *Discourse on Method* (the text which above all legislates for the modern soul) where Descartes affects to deny a certain kind of responsibility for what he is about to do to philosophy:

> So my intention is not to teach here the method which everyone must follow if he is to conduct his reason correctly, but only to demonstrate how I have tried to conduct my own. Those who take responsibility for giving precepts must think themselves more knowledgeable than those to whom they give them, and, if they make a mistake, they are blameworthy. But, putting forward this essay as nothing more than an historical account, or, if your prefer, a fable in which, among certain examples one may follow, one will find also many others which it would be right not to copy, I hope it will be useful to some without being harmful to any, and that my frankness will be well received by all. (*D*, 28-9)

We have come across frankness before, in the concealments of the Pepysian text, and here too it is a ruse. There are at least two ulterior strategies at work in this extraordinary description of the 'philosophical' task. The easy, reasonable tone given throughout to the conversational *persona* who utters the *Discourse* is essentially a device of seduction designed to lure the putative non-philosophical reader on towards the outrageous propositions concerning his body and his soul that Descartes will advance. A guileful democracy of gesture characterizes the text's encoding of its own status, feigning to disavow technical expertise or superior ability, always assuming a genial community of understanding between it and its singular reader. But at the same time this passage is one of many in the text which acknowledge both the censorship which is the positive condition of its discourse (in a sense we have already encountered), and also the less constitutive but no less dangerous ideological censure which Descartes anticipates – rightly – his text will attract. At the moment when he changes fundamentally the structure, style, contents and purposes of philosophy, his text underplays, disingenuously, the authority of its own project. It has even been argued that the *Discourse* as a whole is an alibi, a Trojan horse to smuggle in the concealed advance guard of the scientific work which was for Descartes the centre of his discursive activity (despite our screen memory of him as a philosopher), and whose early publication he abandoned when he heard of the fate of Galileo, who, shown the instruments, recanted . . . . In any case, the disclaimer is there: while no doubt committed to his text, Descartes does not make the strongest of claims for its dangerous truth, but offers it instead as a particular kind of exemplary narrative. But notwithstanding its apparent modesty, which should no longer deceive anyone, especially not those who must still live it, the Cartesian fable depends upon a structure of relations between the entities it conjures up which is not only novel but definitive of the subjectivity it itself inaugurates, as it calls into being within an implicitly censored narration both a reading and a writing subject. From the beginning the text constructs within itself a position for an already-constituted reader capable of distinguishing, as this passage advises it to do, between what is valuable in the *Discourse* and what is error. It incites a reading subject who is already that private and judicious individual whose constitutional location in bourgeois discursivity is elaborated by *Areopagitica*. At the same time as this functions to pre-empt external regulation of the discourse, as in the Miltonic text, by emphasizing the responsibility, the *self-regulation*, of this reader, it also positively constitutes that reading subject under these conditions, establishing it thus as a feature of the legibility of the text as such. Thus the *Discourse* rehearses, unknown to itself, that general shift from violence to 'ideology' as the normative component of domination, by importing censorship into the subject of discourse, the reading subject's capacity for criticism immolated from the start.

The double of this reader, rhetorically bonded to it in the complicity of a shared common sense, which the *Discourse* assumes from its first page to be the inalienable possession of each subject worthy of the name, and the arbiter-medium of all signification, is the subject of the *Discourse* itself: that lonely *ego* which at the crucial step of the argument, the moment of the *cogito*, doubts the existence of everything except its own thinkingness, including even that of its own body. It too must establish itself in place radically wounded, as it demolishes all its former opinions (while complacently deciding to live in the meantime under the laws and manners of its native country, lest this self-aggression seems *revolutionary*) and as it divides itself from itself to become both the subject and the object of its fabular narration. Adrift even from the external world, of whose being it has no certainty, it stabilizes itself by discursive parthenogenesis, inheriting the logic of Hamlet's soliloquy, of which – within the text – it is the sole hearer. But no longer bearing the conditions of a Hamlet, whose generalized speculations on an abstract self – 'What a piece of work is a man...' (II.ii. 301) – were overheard in a full place charged with a density of signification, the Cartesian subject, turning in a vacuum, must round on and penetrate itself as object of its own speech in order to find the moment in an emptied and de-realized world to set its discourse in motion. In Descartes the space of being reduces itself to a single mathematical point from which, as in Pepys, blind to itself, discourse is launched, but where no dynamic is possible without internal fission.

For the subject to apprehend itself as Other, which is the gesture of the Cartesian subject as it recounts the fable of its own subjection, to construct the legend, the readability of its own life, is not an accidental feature of this situation: not least because of the precision of its difference from what preceded its event. The *Discourse*, as an autobiographical account of subjectivity, founds that regularity of subject-centred *and subject-based* discourse which enables the Pepysian text, for all the quotidian density of the latter. In this it separates itself decisively from earlier auto-biographical and biographical texts – mainly hagiographic – in which the account of self was also exemplary, but in quite a different way from that of the Cartesian fable. Such texts propose to demonstrate the workings of a, sometimes mysterious, truth elsewhere; they illustrate the ways of God, whose Truth it was, to men; or more frequently the ways of the recounted self to God: 'Lord, make me chaste, but not yet'. The self is wholly present to itself because its coherence, although not its righteousness, is guaranteed in another, transcendent, place: its ability to recount itself is not, thus, a deep fissure predicating its subjectivity as such, nor the principle of any anxiety. But in the *Discourse* the narrated self becomes for the first time not only the exemplum but the ground of truth. It is only possible for Descartes to reconstruct the external world, and finally prove the existence of God, by traversing the essential instant of the *cogito* where the self's *existence* must be the case on each and every occasion that it asserts it to be so. This constitutive role for the subject, as sharp in definition as it is poverty-stricken in its certainty, is quite distinct from the earlier discipline of autobiographical discourse which inhabited an ontologically and epistemologically simpler world, where the sure and – in principle – easily accessible grounds of truth and being were apprehended as exterior to the subject: the problem then was an ethical one for the fallible saints and we others, not of having to live the Law, but only to live *by* it.

The Cartesian text does its historical work in its form and its discursive strategies more than in the detail of its argument (for one might refute the proofs of the existence of God and leave the structure of subjectivity it discloses intact). It constitutes the bourgeois individual as a split narration isolated within a censored discourse where it is crucial both that it is narrated and that it is censored. In doing so it also establishes the subjectivity which is later to be analysed in that other record of modernity, the Freudian text, where, too, narration is of the essence – whether it be in the recounting of Freud's auto-analysis, the first person disposition which so frequently shapes the report of his conceptual discoveries in others, or in the case-histories where, because the neurotic subject's inner controls have failed, the authority of a master-narrator, legitimated by science, must be invoked in order to objectify the subject in such a way that it can assume its subjectivity again. (Dora, of course, walked out.) If Freudian narration differs from Descartes in a number of its philosophical assumptions, it is nevertheless inconceivable outside the field of the Cartesian inauguration. Attempts have been made, despite this, to eternalize Freud; in particular the sexual base which is said to provide the endstop of the Freudian explanatory model (although Freud himself believed that analysis was interminable) has been vulgarized into an abiding naturalism. This has led both to the necessarily inconclusive 'debate' between a certain Marxist historicism and a psychoanalytic anthropologism, and also to such immense and usually obscure theoretical efforts of resocialization that even the self-regard of a Jacques Lacan could barely encompass the task. But it is worth reflecting that while the sexual insistence should not be set aside, for in one sense it accurately reflects the new status of the post-Cartesian, post-Pepysian body, at least those other Freudian figures given in the joke, the parapraxis and the dream, should be brought into substantive focus as the appropriate devices of the discourse of bourgeois subjectivity that is Freud's *historical* starting place and object. Not, as we have seen in Pepys, simply a sexual *repression* (although bourgeois subjectivity is redolent with the metaphysic of interiority, incipient in the Oedipal prince and elaborated since) but strategies of *complex discourse*, for which there is no explanatory limit other than the descriptively given extensiveness of textuality itself. The decisive outline of this subjectivity, in the essence of its representation (as opposed to its external social and political organization), is the pattern of obliquity, evasion, displacement and condensation which we have seen at work in the incorporeal speech of a private writer.

The text of Pepys' *Diary* counts the cost of the Cartesian intervention and the restructuration of life it signals, and we can also determine there, finally, the fate of that citizen for whose civil liberty Milton had argued in *Areopagitica*. For one thing he is quite mad. The structure of Pepys' discourse conforms exactly to – choosing one example among many possible, for what is important is the splitting and not the precise shape of the model – R. D. Laing's semi-theoretical diagram of the schizoid subject. In both a public *persona* surrounds an intermediate self (of which neither are 'really' the subject's own, just as the *Diary* tries to say that the part of Pepys that consumes the pleasures of the French text is not *really* Pepys); and within these there shelters a disembodied 'inner self': in the case of Pepys, the I that writes the text. But if the pertinent image of sanity is that self-possessed Reason which Descartes counter-poses, as an absolute and unbridgeable opposite, to the madness he excludes from the trials which natural or intellectual doubt must submit itself to; or if it is the sober judgement with which Milton endows the private subject, clearly neither describes the Pepysian situation, except in the complex sense that the transactions of the text can be read as the mark and the place of the struggle and the splitting necessary to secure that rational serenity at one level of the soul, as it contains and interns its delinquent others. But in doing so it accedes to the other madness Laing diagnoses. The passage of 9 February 1668 describes the play of still-unstable energies as the bourgeois

58

citizen-subject, constituted in its area of private freedom, is made to work, as Althusser said, 'all by itself'. No longer mainly to be licensed by the state – in any of the senses possible here – the subject becomes self-censoring. The I that writes deletes *from its own text* the body of the unacceptable, or allots it to a marginal or parenthetical status (of which the supervening I is, as they say, 'unconscious') but from which it none the less threatens to return.

The constitution of the subject in this form is the principal support of the new order. Its splitting, in which modern discourse is founded, engenders that intense self-'consciousness' (which occurring prematurely in Hamlet could only be an embarrassment to those around him). It imbues a moment of the subject, to one side of the split, with an awareness of self that goes along with the elision from that consciousness of other elements of the psychic ensemble, from, that is, the subject's total discourse. At the very moment when the I can begin to be used transitively, it is already to one side of a division which separates it from other meanings and urgencies which the narrating and narrated selves struggle to exclude and ignore, and register but obliquely, although they are the conditions of the elements which *are* accessible to the apparently self-possessed consciousness. The splitting of the subject, within which the self as present to itself is only one moment, and the charged reflexivity of that moment, is the point of purchase within the subject of its subjection. The profound and corporeal guilt with which the subject is invested as the febrile undertone of that self-consciousness, which turns out to know so little of itself, is decisive in securing the deep inner control, which has been called interpellation, that is so vital to the bourgeois illusion of freedom in its civil and its personal guises. It always-already prejudices the independence of the free subject, short-circuiting that subject's potentially subversive desire by establishing inside it a self-disciplinary fixation predicated on the outlawing of the body and its passions as the absolute outside, for the discourse of the subject in its principle of deployment, of the consciousness and the 'unconsciousness' – although not of the existence – of the divided subject. It draws a shifting but unbreakable limit around subjectivity as the domain of propriety and speech, not as a code of manners (as if the Pepysian text were more than superficially about social life in that sense), but as a deep structural effect of this form of the subject's locatedness in being and signification.

But even to speak of this device of domination as *control* is already to suggest a degree of externality false to the efficiency of this modern subjection. While it would be difficult to deny that external controls are at work in bourgeois society, and never more so than when the crisis of these societies breaks the fragile consensus which is their 'natural' form and spawns the intensified activity of the more tangible agents of the state, both armed and 'ideological', this must not occlude for us the more profound strategy of domination which is achieved not by *post hoc* intervention from without, but by the pre-constitution of the subject in its subjection. The subject is cast in on itself, controlled from within by its selves; crippled by struggles and anxieties inside itself; radically undermined by the loss of its own body with which it is ever in contact but whose insistent reminders of a material limit to its subjection, which it cannot quite determine for itself, it must ever attempt to quell. Or more efficiently still, the subject is constituted in its consciousness unconscious of those anxieties and that loss, in a condition we know as health, reason and conformity: health despite our sickness; reason despite our madness; and conformity despite the allowed and enforced discords which, within and between us, separate each of us from the more devastating – revolutionary – treachery to this system of presence we should have to live out if we are to survive our subjection.

When Descartes, whose discourse also layers feint within feint, installs the new sovereign within the inner kingdom of the subject itself, he banishes madness by fiat (as Foucault reminds us) from his argument and his texts:

> And how could I deny that these hands and this body belong to me, unless perhaps I were to assimilate myself to those insane persons whose minds are so troubled

and clouded by the black vapours of the bile that they constantly assert that they are kings, when they are very poor; that they are wearing gold and purple, when they are quite naked; or who imagine . . . that they have a body of glass. But these are madmen, and I would not be less extravagant if I were to follow their example. (M, 96)

By rejecting that extravagance, Descartes also pre-determines – not by 'philosophy' but by textual gesture – that already the subject which utters and is uttered in the *Meditations* is not and cannot be insane, whatever other doubts it will have to circumvent in establishing itself in its subjectivity. But the reason to which that madness is the opposite is no simple category of philosophical or even psychological demonstration, but a token, as its metaphors reveal, of the entire political order within which it emerges and which the Cartesian text ciphers. The unknown wager historically at stake in this manoeuvre, at the beginning of the epoch it founds, is that one day, at its end, those who have the temerity to accede to that madness which might assert that it is better to be sovereign than to be very poor, or to be dressed in gold and purple than to be naked, will not organize themselves – not beyond all rationality, but beyond this Reason – to dispossess the *bourgeois* philosopher-king from the calm order of his self-representation and from his magistracy in the discursive regime articulating and articulated by it. Even at the risk of appearing to reason and common sense, those Cartesian doubles, as so deranged that they imagine their bodies to be made of glass.

It is decisive, especially against the diverse reception of the two texts – one within philosophy, or ideology in its purest form, and the other on the margins of literature – that Descartes and Pepys approximate so closely to each other in the rhetoric of common sense which provides in both the alibi of the evasion of censorship from without and within. The understated gesture of these texts is that which simply writes down what has happened, what the self has thought, seen or done, *as if* without consequence. And yet the covert proximity of this international common sense to the erasure of the body, as the new order establishes both its philosophical and its more mundane discourse, will now appear accidental only on pain of ignoring what it was itself constructed to ignore. It begins to insist at the exact moment when the modern body assumes its parenthetical status, and flows into the vacancy in being left behind after the withdrawal from the limitless limits which had previously held. The Cartesian and the Pepysian equality of common sense, the one stated and the other implied as the epistemological gesture of the text's discourse, matches that other democracy of corporeal elision by which the body politic of all is fractured and reorganized until it devolves into the private body of each. In this condition, apparently beyond reckoning, it sinks beneath the discursivity of the subject who is now author, and is absented from its signification; while common sense, the initial legislator and then the inheritor of this settlement, gathers all facticity to its own propositionless, incontrovertible, but bodiless speech. For if the text of Pepys is troubled by anxieties it can hardly name, if it is invested and reinvested by evasions which nevertheless articulate themselves in and around the discourse of the clerk as he sings with his friends under the shadow of *L'escholle des filles*, read only for information's sake, it is because of the tremulous existence of the modern body which is spoken there at the same time as it is silenced. Constituted *in writing*, the discursive medium which governs the epoch and separates itself silently but efficiently from the spectacle, covering its own traces, the bourgeois subject substitutes for its corporeal body the rarefied body of the text. Even the guilty sexuality which the passage takes such pains not to speak, and thus speaks the more clearly, derives not from another body but from the French text, which as a text, and as this particular text, represents a certain bodily existence which cannot now itself be other than a representation. The carnality of the body has been dissolved and dissipated until it can be reconstituted in writing at a distance from itself. As the subject, in a private condition, writes, from that blind place within which it is necessarily blind in order to see, of necessity censored in order to write, it unfolds itself now within a mode of representation which is no longer of a substance with the materiality of the old body. As the flesh is de-realized, representation, which becomes at last representational, is separated from it and puts in train a mode of signification for which, to borrow a word from Derrida, the body has become supplementary. Neither wholly present, nor wholly absent, the body is confined, ignored, exscribed from discourse, and yet remains at the edge of visibility, troubling the space from which it has been banished.

The modern body is forced down in front of discourse where it cannot realize incarnationally the central significations which the older body, in all its painful exactitude, was able to bear out; and not just because those meanings in a new age are now different, but because it is also a transformed and relocated body. Before this inception of the new order and of modern subjectivity, the flesh was the immediate, the unmediated, site of desire and penalty. Judicial torture bore down on it, and the mortification of the flesh was merely the starkest form of an ethic which never had to divide itself: the ancient pseudo-separation of the body and the soul, scourging one to liberate the other (an endeavour whose impossibility was given in the saintly beatitude of its few successes), was predicated on their real inseparability. But in the Pepysian situation, as the body and the book separate in the writing of the subject, desire and meaning have become detached from each other so that in the end Freudian analysis will have to seek out either the meaning of every desire or behind every meaning the desire which is not fully present in its expression. If, before this eventuality analysis of the soul did not take that Freudian form, it was not because there was no 'primitive' psychology (although, in the theory of the humours, the *anatomy* of melancholy, it was thoroughly corporeal); nor because 'development' had not yet taken things to the panicky modern threshold beyond which its ministrations would be, as they say, needed; but because the body had not yet been divided structurally from the meanings which such analysis would later have to attempt to return to it. The gap did not exist for analysis to cross, for only the ambivalent modern body could be party to such a tortuous exchange.

The supplementary body is both more present and more absent than the old body: its urgency has been divided. On one hand its dangerous passions have been contained and, by disarticulation and interiorization, made to contribute, as the guilt of the split subject, to those anxieties which undermine it from within and secure its subjection. This deleterious moment of the modern body is not present to the subject as a direct principle of its discourse, but merely as a residual energy, an absent principle of the textuality in which the new subjectivity articulates itself. As the Pepysian text demonstrates, the body and its passions are at work in and around the portions of the discourse in which the subject is present to itself, but only as the effects of a guilty evasion, a turning aside uttered by the subject but in an important sense unknown to it. On the other hand, as a material limit, the body cannot be jettisoned entirely: on the contrary, it must be fitted for that disciplined and recurrent labour which the emergent capitalist economy will deploy with increasing scope and intensity. But this other aspect of the modern body, which we shall examine later in the surprising return to the Cartesian text – under the form of a repressive health – of the very corporeality which at the moment of absolute subjectivity had had to be expelled from it, cannot be present to itself either; it cannot *itself* signify, but becomes an object *for* discursive practice, present to discourse only across the distance of representation. But here, in Pepys, it is the first aspect of this body, its discursive 'absence' (which is also *that* object-'presence'), which is foremost as the text distributes itself around the reduced but troubling corporeality its speech acknowledges and denies.

The passage from the *Diary* celebrates the pathos of this body, and of this situation. Reaching out to arrest the world, it is perpetually debilitated by that frustrated drive towards nostalgic plenitude whose object can now be glimpsed only

64

in the strategies of a writing whose diversion from its own goal is its organizational principle. It is a body cast into marginality, lost between the lines of the subject's discourse which, while purporting to describe everyday things in a plain style, can never free itself from the deficiency that the quotidian density hides from it. The difficulties that characterize the life of this man are nowhere more eloquently or movingly spoken than in the compulsive return of the text to the site of the body from which it departs, to rumours of the body and its passions and functions, to representations that mark out an absence which the body-of-the-text will never supply. As the subject's discourse constructs itself ever more palpably, depending for its substance on the concretion of the object-world, the more insistently is it constrained to grasp at this other materiality which it cannot apprehend. Parasitic on the body it scorns, it tries to fill the space of being as if it were a full space, but only on the mournful condition that this hollowing of its disembodied text is unknown to it.

In this of its aspects the body lingers just beyond the limits of discourse, in so far as the subject's speech is present to itself. It hovers outside the charmed circle of subjective self-possession, and from that boundary position continues to agitate the order within the perimeter. But as the passage shows, that position is also an inner limit which divides the subject's speech from itself, so that the discourse of the clerk, arranged around as well as against the body, must therefore police the interior as well as the frontiers against its restless energy, its lack. As we have seen, the text's internal protocols are deployed to segregate and displace acknowledgement of the desiring body which the subject can no longer recognize as fully its own, but must disavow, translate, or consume as representation. In this agonized predicament, in which the subject is thrust into a spurious self-recognition – as the price and not the triumph of this form of subjectivity – the body plays a part only as the denied other of the soul in whose order it has become a detritus on a level with those other Others whom the Great Confinement expelled and interned in the same action. As the novel strategy of textual ostracization is substituted for the old violence of the spectacle, the body is allotted to a subordination which, beyond the pale of civility, might well have appeared – even then – as dangerously renegade if it were not for the relative consistency of the subject's self-apparency. But when it is recognized at all by this form of the subject's discourse, the body is admitted only as a nameless momentum outside the real arena of meaning and endeavour, as an unruly mess of functions and afflictions which only in its object-aspect will discourse be able to name, categorize and subdue. Short of that medicalization, whose Cartesian inception in the precise context of the constitution of the subject we have already referred to, the body in the Pepysian text is no more than a monstrous, residual irrationality which has had to be expelled from discourse at least in so far as the subject experiences itself as initiator of its own speech. It is a sickly body, and passionate but without spirituality. It is bereft of ethical value (except as denial and negation), and its value in the market-place still awaits a suitable calculus to determine it: even then, as the muted violence of the *Diary* repeatedly insists, it must never again be admitted to the new order of presence from which it has been excluded.

But even as the body is dispatched to the outer and inner limits of visibility it takes on a charge which is less dramatic than that of the old body, but none the less powerful for being so. If the new settlement is one of wretched pathos for the subject, this is engendered at least in part by the revenge of the formless body as it subverts, from within, the morality, the complacency and the textuality of the subject. Because no form of power is total (although there may be *one* exception to this), for without resistance there can be no domination but merely non-contradictory stasis, the body continues to exercise a disturbing influence even where it is absent. It is clear from the Pepysian text that although it is an early instance of the new regime, a continual effort will be needed to keep the new subjectivity efficient, and the body in its place. As the anxieties at work here testify, an uneasy equilibrium at best holds between the component moments of the situation (especially because the productive and reproductive body is needed as much as the desiring body must be reduced to quiescence), and an ever-present threat of insurrection by the body against the soul will have to characterize the successive recensions of the bourgeois settlement as it mutates through time. An early text of that settlement, Pepys is also a first graph of struggle within the order, the text of a certain potential for instability and transfiguration.

For the moment, however, we must see in it the essential outline of the liaisons between subjectivity, discourse and the body which make up in promissory form the regime which was conceived in the seventeenth century and has matured since then. As the privatized subject writes, its text is constrained to say more than it knows itself to say, an excess of signification beyond the self's lived disposition which is incited, paradoxically, by the censorship which is the governing principle of its discourse. The split subject is designed at an abject inner distance from itself and from the ambivalent, supplementary body which has been exiled, in one of its aspects, from the interior consistency of the subject's discourse to a ghostly, insubstantial place at the margins, and in its other phase, to a location outside discourse as one amongst its objects in the world. To discourse is now to live; this body is beyond the limit.

Disinherited and separated, the body is traduced as a rootless thing of madness and scandal; and then finally, in its object-aspect, it is pressed into service.

From that crowded chamber in which Hamlet was the observ'd of all observers, to introject the incorporeal subject into that other, silent, empty chamber where the ciphered text of the *Diary* is written in anguish and complacency at the same, mutually ignorant, instants: the two chambers figure the scope of the reorganization of life which was effected across the revolutionary years. Signification is now no longer the spectacularity of meaning and error deployed across the surface of a violent but full plenum, but a shadowy half-presence furtively enunciated and consumed in a bedroom and an office where it is fixed in restless motion. The privacy of the second chamber throws into sharp relief the visibilities of the first and describes, for the seventeenth century, the destination of the narrative, although a point of departure for ourselves. But this should be said carefully. Neither of these moments should be conceived teleologically, for just as not every beginning is an Origin, so not every outcome is a teleological goal. It is not as though everything that went before Pepys had to lead to this text, to this discursivity. Still less can it function in respect of ourselves as a once and for all determination of unalterable consequence, but rather as a cardinal point of self-understanding which can only be identified by virtue of that hindsight which is no more than the capacity to fashion here a genesis for some of our own conditions and dilemmas.

To construct the story of this past is to pay some of the price that continues to be exacted for what was done to us in the seventeenth century, which, as the examples of Pepys and Descartes adequately show, confirmed by the Freudian return, made narration of us all. Even as the compulsion to narrate subjects us, it holds us back from another madness which post-modernism – that ultra-leftism of the spirit – recommends when, in offering to reject all narrative, it jettisons what can only count in our epoch as sense itself. Describing this mode of our subjection entails a recognition that we are part of the discursive history that made us, even as we struggle to overcome it; a recognition that there is no simple outside to this power, as ultra-leftism must always assume there to be, but only the possibility of fabricating other narratives which will counter-value the dominant story, history, whose greatest achievement has been to conceal its own fictionality. If the radical counter-narration, operating athwart the master-text, can expose that devisedness to view – the better.

Enough of the past is lost, and looks in any case so different from different points of vantage, for all history to be regarded as no more (and indeed *no less*) than a present fiction which must be constructed obliquely or directly according to the often only half-apprehended order of contemporary needs and struggles. Not everything in the seventeenth century led inexorably to Pepys: it is enough that it now leads to this text-man, alone in his chamber with his discourse and his sex; raging, solitary, productive.

INTO
THE
VAULT

The body was too coarse to feel the utmost of
our sorrows and our joys. Therefore, we abandoned
it as rubbish: we left it below us to march forward,
a breathing simulacrum, on its own unaided level,
subject to influences from which in normal times
our instincts would have shrunk. (T.E. Lawrence, *Seven
Pillars of Wisdom*)

In Rembrandt's *The Anatomy Lesson of Dr. Nicolaas Tulp*, the gaze of a certain male science, no doubt in its infancy as they say, is organized around a seventeenth-century body which has already become ambiguous. Its neck broken, the corpse of *het Kint* lies obliquely within the frame of an image that is redolent of the vicissitudes of the body as it traverses and is traversed by the history of subjection which we now inherit. The chest is thrust forward in *rigor mortis*: Adriaan Adriaanszoon, also known as Aris Kint, is less than thirty-six hours dead (*H*, 36, 131). A life has just been extinguished; but a body is being made to signify, and to signify according to a mode of representation to which the body is only accessible on pain of a kind of death, actual for this petty thief from Leiden, more comprehensively – and more literally – exercised by the regime of subjection which is beginning to be practised in this painting.

But is it not perverse to locate a reading of this image within the problematics of the hollowed, double, modern body, when surely everything about it assigns the painting to the old theatre of corporal torment, to the Jacobean spectacle of the full body *in extremis*? Does not the very *mise en scène* disclose a proximity not to the decorporealized discourse of a Pepys, but to the overt, celebratory bodiliness of the dramatic and penal scaffold? It is, after all, a ghastly tableau, close to tragedy, which was in fact produced in a theatre in Amsterdam before an audience who had paid for their tickets, who stand where we stand as we observe the painting, and whom the anatomist Tulp, his left hand raised in indication of speech, addresses across this public body. Is he not then as much the agent of an older punishment as the representative of a novel science? Does not the annual public dissection, conducted with solemn and awful ritual in the depth of winter, merely extend the execution which immediately preceded it and which provides its patient; and isn't this festive, instructive and minatory performance – which, at most, we might regard as some fusion of punishment and science – then completed by the commemorative banquet for the Guild of Surgeons by which it is followed? To execute, to dismember, to eat. It is difficult to imagine how much more thorough than this an act of corporal punishment could be.

Enlightened voices were already beginning to be raised, even in the early seventeenth century, against the penal character of the public dissections, before a major ideological shift in the strategies of power permitted them fully to be heard (*H*, 105). But both the sparsity and the insistence of those protests serve to emphasize how close these ceremonies still were, for all that they point forward to a modern, surgical regime of the body, to the previous and still contemporary scenes of corporal penalty at which the power of the sovereign pursued the flesh of the transgressor beyond death itself. There clings to them the aura and much of the moral sanction of the scaffold on which, if necessary, the last particle of the body was made to yield up its recompense for a transgression which could not be rehabilitated but only extirpated completely. Tulp's instruments, thus, if not exactly the tools of judicial torture, are manipulated none the less with a dexterity – and, above all, a semiotic precision – which is cognate with the techniques of judicious pain. If the *hand* of a thief, as the offending member, would receive the special attention of the executioner, no less does it here receive the first ministrations of the anatomist, against, as it turns out, the protocols, logic and custom of every other didactic anatomy of the period. It is not to the order of science or pedagogy that this first incision refers, but rather it is a meaningful episode within a complete drama of retribution whose second act Rembrandt depicts in his painting (*H*, 33). The scene of dissection is thus the exercise of a jurisdiction over the body of Aris Kindt, an act of penal and sovereign domination which is exemplary and substantive, symbolic and material, at one and the same time. It searches out in dramatic and public fashion, and then realizes, corporal meanings which belong to a disposition of power that is fully committed to the wholly present body of the old regime of signification. Viewed in this way the scene portrayed in Rembrandt's painting belongs historically more to the undivided plenum of the spectacularity of meaning that surrounds Hamlet, than to the riven condition of modern subjectification offered within the prince, the condition under which the divided body has been distanced from the plane of discourse to return only as a symptomatic disturbance on the one hand, and an objectified brutality on the other.

But if these registers are there in the painting, it is necessary today to excavate them from a canvas which would otherwise appeal for its essential meanings solely to the history of science (and to an early development in the claimed realism of bourgeois representation). And in a sense rightly so, if it is detached from the performative context to which the hand of the surgeon gestures. Were it not for those spectators, whom we who now look unwittingly become, the picture would indeed be less ambiguous, less historically nuanced than it is. Without that reminder of the public setting of this ritual dissection, the surface of the painting would lack the duality by which it now acts as both a suture and a break between the old plenitude of corporeal retribution which is its residual component, and emergent themes of another and perhaps more deadly science which it also strives to depict. It would lose the axis of *difference* by which at the same time as the gruesome ceremony which was enacted in the anatomy theatre in the *Waaggebouw* during those January nights in 1632 summons up the spectacular corporeality of a polity that signalized itself in a bodily density far more incandescent than that of this corpse on a dissecting table, it also gave rise to the now more clearly visible modernity of the painting which marked Rembrandt's entry as a fashionable painter into *bourgeois* society and which, moreover, exemplifies and adorns what was to be for a long period the official art of that society.

Aesthetically and ideologically the painting is a palimpsest, layering one set of encratic signs upon another. If Tulp is an agent of pain, he also extracts a recompense of surgical information. Even if the chair in which he sits, dimly visible behind him, is placed on the site of the old throne from which the fiat of corporal obliteration had been uttered, the master of the body is now installed in the seat of civil government and authoritative learning. The power of

Tulp's world is not that of the old kingdom, but nor has it quite erased the traces of that older sovereignty: rather, it seeks to take them over, to appropriate the ancient vengeful motifs and to rearticulate them for its own new purposes. The image fashions an aesthetic which is rationalistic, classical, realistic, but one to which the iconography of a previous mode of representation that symbolized more than it depicted is not completely alien; medical but still inextricably connected with the earlier pageant of sacramental violence. If it continues to evoke the signs of a punitive corporeality no longer quite appropriate to the republic of property it was made to epitomize, if it contains still a – newly barbaric – reference to defeated transgression and to penal revenge exercised on the body of the transgressor, it also aims to draw off and reorganize the charge of those potent residues, and to invest them, transformed, in a moment of hygienic science which will soon free itself entirely from the old body, even if it trades at first on the mystique and the terror of that abandoned materiality.

The historical transformation which lies behind the palimpsestic impaction is not, however, evenly active in the image, and it is the modernizing pole of its dialectic which is dominant and therefore 'spontaneously' visible today. From this perspective, of course, the painting celebrates not the body of Aris Kindt (which none the less finds its last significance here) but the presence of the surgeons who attend Tulp's demonstration. If the painting's aesthetic is a realism, its social valency is given in those grave bourgeois faces, avid or complacent, which stare across and out of the frame. They too are strangely paradoxical: on the threshold of an epistemological journey into the modern, and yet frozen eternally in a solidarity of prestige, learning and prosperity (although the fact that each had paid to be present in the depiction may only serve to make us unduly cynical about the inner principle of a such a collectivity). They represent at once new historical movement, and its hypostatization, for, stylistically in touch with the plethora of other group portraits in which this bourgeoisie, in its first ascendancy, celebrated and had represented its own solidity – as epistemological as it is political and social – the painting seeks to portray not merely some random scene, some historical anecdote (although any realism must always run this risk) but an episode charged with the semiosis of the new power, represented, however, as an already achieved, and indeed eternal fact. If the backward masses who look on are present at some bloody ceremony, we, these gentle faces say, oblivious of the dialectic, are present in the name of the rational spirit of a capitalism which is able to represent itself here, in those faces, as enlightened, liberal and confident. Less troubled than Pepys, less angry than Milton, these surgeons, who are the brothers of *Areopagitica*'s self-disciplining citizen, are also the spiritual allies of the rationalistic philosopher who sheltered in their city from the political struggles of his own country, and who may well have been present at this dissection: that 'avid amateur anatomist', Descartes himself (*H*, 26).

But with what philosophical serenity, identical to that with which, in similar paintings, the regents and governors of the multiplicity of houses of confinement which grew up in Amsterdam in greater numbers and earlier than anywhere else, embody their authority, are those gazes able not to perceive the violent act of domination upon which this painting, almost despite itself, predicates their tranquility? It would perhaps be too humanistic now to refer this blindness to the status of a joke on Rembrandt's part (although as a painter who was so frequently condemned by other artists for associating with the lower orders, who mixed with *Jews*, who went bankrupt in an age of accumulation, he was located somewhat ironically, shall we say, within the social order he depicts), but the fact remains: no eye within the painting sees the body. The scientific gaze, the perspective of natural philosophy, may be organized around the corpse, but in order not to see it. The lines of sight can be easily traced. They return from the surgeons to we who look (how real we are), or they run to the anatomy atlas open at the foot of the corpse. Only Jacob Koolvelt, the surgeon on the extreme left of the painting (who, with Frans van Loenen at the top of the central triangle of figures, was painted in at a later date, not only unbalancing Rembrandt's composition, but also betraying again the doubtful principle of solidarity which founds this 'group'), and Tulp himself break the pattern; and then only to reinforce it by equally failing to see what Rembrandt, in a radical departure in the organization of anatomy paintings hitherto, has placed so prominently in view. That, in particular, the eyes of surgeons Mathys Kalkoen, Jacob de Witt and Jacob Blok (third, fourth and fifth from the right) are focused not on the body but on the text is something we shall have to return to; but that even they do not see the flesh, tantalizing as the proximity of their lines of sight to it is, only further emphasizes the extraordinary historical contortion by which this body on display has become in an important sense invisible. In the mode of its now brute materiality, thus reduced, the body has ceased to mean in any but residual ways, sinking away from vision into the past.

But it is discarded in the moment it is transformed. For in another modality a part of this body has, of course, been readmitted to the charmed circle where signification is possible, even if only on pain of yet further a set of transformations beyond the mere – and for these scientists, apparently casual – extinction of life. The left forearm and hand, the very limb which in Tulp signifies speech, has begun to find the proper form of a new and more acceptable corporeality. Science has revealed the structure beneath its surface, and has already produced in it the rarefied, reductive simplicity of the empiricist distinction between the core of useful meaning and the waste phenomenon. The abstracting operation by which modern knowledge will master the flesh, even at this more or less initial moment, emerges in the painting at the very point where Tulp's forceps, and the social relations of domination they mediate, transform the corpse of Aris Kindt into a resource for epistemic processing. But at this early moment, the incision is achieved at the cost of some disturbance to the decorum of the painting: if not an *aporia* at least a reflex of the involution necessary to bring this departure into effect. Despite the dense 'realism' perennially attributed to the painting's semiotic mode, it is already profoundly unrealistic in content in so far as no anatomy of the period ever began with the dissection of the hand, but with the opening of the *venter inferior* and removal of the viscera which were most prone to rapid putrefaction (*H*, 132). And the representation of the dissected hand disrupts the mode itself, the form of the signification which is supposed to guarantee the apparency, the facticity of the bourgeois world. Not only is the left arm of the corpse grossly over-large (the foreshortening of the otherwise careful depth-giving perspective should have the more distant arm shorter than the nearer one, even allowing for elongation due to the incision and flaying) but in addition it is anatomically inaccurate. The tendons revealed belong not to the palm of the left hand – the position of thumb indicates that the hand is palm upwards – but to the back of the right (*H*, 66). If the dominant discourse of the picture gives us the real as we have been taught to perceive it (that massive ideological operation by which bourgeois discourse naturalizes what it has itself constructed as reality, truistically educating the perceptions towards ratification of what is thus circularly obvious), the diagram of the hand which has been superimposed by Rembrandt on a body evidently drawn as Heckscher ingenuously remarks 'from life' (*H*, 66), while seeking that apparency in its highest, most 'scientific' form, veers away into what is by its own terms of reference cross error. And by other terms of reference corporeal anxiety. The crude diagram, taken perhaps from one of the anatomy atlases visible in the painting, in striving to confirm that this new facticity masters not only the surface, but according to a new metaphysic the depths as well, discloses aesthetic – and because of the painting's ideologically totalizing objectives, ideological – debility: athwart the unity of its realism lie marks of the torsions and the self-betrayal of an ethic of salient domination for which coherence, objectivity, rationality are otherwise watchwords. That the betrayal finds its affective device and its substantial location in the representation of a damaged body is now unsurprising.

But it is in this way that the corpse of Aris Kindt, for all the painting's quotation of the old visuality, becomes indeed the modern flesh, the doubleness of which is given in the failure of the image to achieve a unified painterly discourse of the body, in its distance from the Jacobean spectacle. Between the greenish, extinct corpse that is universally ignored and the – Cartesian – diagram of the hand is a fissure into which a domination more fundamental than that of the old order has delved, dividing not only the soul from the flesh, but separating within the flesh itself the body as dead residue and the body as the object of a science which in knowing it will master it, and in healing it will accommodate it to labour and docility. On the one hand the dumb flesh, and on the other the mechanism, which can be understood, repaired and made to work. Both of these bodies have now been banished to the other side of the distance *across which* representation must now take place, expelled from the place of signification to the object status of what is signified, and both correspond to aspects of a total fantasy of order which the modern separations we have been charting inaugurate and attempt definitively to secure. In the dead corpse the delinquent passions have been extinguished. The troublesome corporeality which still haunts none the less Pepys' text, is here offered in a moribund carcass the image of its complete erasure and even of its promissory exculpation. The corpse of the thief becomes, unseen, the absent aspect of the modern body, from which the gaze and the trajectory of discourse are averted. And yet at the same time that diagrammatic hand corresponds to what we have called the present aspect of the new body, the corporal moment which, also distanced across the gulf of representation, is sanitized and then reinscribed; at a remove from the absent corporal moment, but equally reduced, changed both in form and palpability.

This modern division-and-rule of the corporal operates across the painting and across its subsequent dispersion a dual strategy in respect of the body: of exclusion – of blindness – and of *textualization*. For those eyes which do not reach outward narcissistically for the returning gaze of the spectator are indeed focused on the text. The painting elaborates a Pepysian figuration of its own as those sight-lines glance off the surface of the body and search out meaning in texts where already the body has been transmuted by representation into an abstraction. There the flesh is indeed being made word. The painting organizes, beside its complex bifurcation and traduction of the body, icons and instances of the newer scriptural industry whose emergence over the rigours and the play of the Jacobean plenum we have already noticed. It marks off against the newly invisible corpse an order of discourse of whose intense textuality, in lieu of a lost bodiliness, Pepys is only one of the earliest pioneers.

But although the project of the image is clearly the textualization given in the uncanny aversion of the surgeons' gaze, as in its other dimensions it would be wrong at this early stage in the process to resolve the painting wholly into the modern discursivity figured in that substitution of text for body. If the body of the painting is ambivalent, so too is the status of the various texts which litter the image. Perhaps here too there is some deconstructive hesitation in the way in which they also offer to equivocate between one historical register of sense and another. The folio anatomy atlas in the bottom right-hand corner of the canvas, which punctuates the line of the corpse and imprisons it within the frame, itself points in two directions. In one respect it refers back to the scholasticism of medieval anatomy under which the *praelector* would pronounce the lesson direct from the text of authority without having himself examined a body, or without a corpse even being available for examination (*H*, 41). But in another respect it points forward to that modern aversionary textualization of the flesh which we have just invoked by recalling the name of Pepys. Or perhaps the oscillation between those two quite different stations of the text – as primal authority on the one hand, and as a record of apparently objective and empirical investigation on the other – may have something of the quality of another Rembrandtian joke. Certainly there is an ironic, if not subversive, movement in the establishment of a connotative

81

identity between these two historical poles: for does it not serve to imply that these scientists, newly committed to a regime of truth which grounds itself in the unalterable factuality of the empirically given, are, unknown to themselves, as much ensnared within the authority of discourse itself – even if, as it were, unconsciously – as their medieval predecessors who at least made no bones about the textual location and bookish form of their knowledge? It is not so much that modernity invents script, but rather that it masks the scripting of what it takes to be real. The unmediated contact with actual reality – that dream and weapon of bourgeois philosophy and common sense alike – turns out, in Rembrandt's deployment of this book of the body, to be as illusory as the corporeal tranquillity which the Pepysian text seeks but fails to find: the depicted calm of these bourgeois surgeons is predicated on an imperception; a moment of new sight is purchased, as we have seen, by blindness. It is thus in its self-representation alone that bourgeois discourse achieves the fresh and innocent pursuit of the real after the mystification of the Schools, the new instrumentality of signification rather than the earlier interference of the palpability of the older discourse which is not being so allegedly transparent, was also not strictly representational either. Just as the painting's realism is shown to be faulty, the instrumentality of scientific discourse is depicted here, in an early form, not as the naked perception and unmediated reproduction of reality, but, unconscious to itself, the produced – and productive – operation of newer codes: not, at last, the Truth, but a new organization of truth within a novel, textuated arrangement of corporeality, subjectivity and the sovereign liaisons of mutual prophylaxis now to govern them.

The archaeological quality of the painting's texts is given also, most graphically *and* most literally, in the sheet of paper which Hartman Hartmansz. hold in *his* left hand. For many years this script was intelligible only as a register, a list of names – common in such commemorative, subscription paintings – of the surgeons depicted. The painting was eventually hung in the anatomy theatre itself, and it must have seemed natural that, to their lasting fame, these literal signs of the surgeons' identities should be recorded along with the image of their faces: they had each, it is true, paid a substantial amount of money for these traces. But, as with so much that is 'natural', all is not what it appears to be. It transpires that these names have been overpainted onto an earlier surface of the image, and when the canvas was cleaned it became clear that beneath them, as part of the first depiction, is yet another diagrammatic representation of the tendons of the arm and hand. Hartmansz. holds, it turns out, not a sheet of paper but a further open anatomy atlas, the left-hand page of which is visible, the right being hidden by the body of the anatomist (H, 14, 67-70, 133). But if not 'original', yet with what analytic accuracy – doubtless again unconscious – did that second seventeenth-century hand when it sought a place for this writing superimpose it precisely there, especially when a site is already prepared for it on the *affiche* which hangs in the background – presumably announcing the dissection in whose depiction it appears (H, 11) – on which Rembrandt's signature and the date of the painting are clearly to be seen. With what tragic modern percipience, no doubt also afflicted with the complex blindness in play across this image, did that other painter, who was perhaps Rembrandt himself, seek the identity of these men in their names, and then inscribe that nomenclature, palimpsestically, on the representation of the body which one of them holds. For between these two layered surfaces there is an equivocation which manifests in particularly poignant form the rigours of the modern organization of subjectivity. If anything that is is identical with itself, then it is only by the thinnest of margins that these two registers of being *fail* to coalesce. Unidentical with each other, these two layers – the represented corporeal and the literal marks of identity – are held apart by the minute distance and difference that signal their reciprocal alienation. Between them is the caesura which not only detaches the modern subject from the body, but ensures that in its very identity it is not what it is: a non-identical identity insists, no more than provisionally secured by the merest smear of paint, which then buries, in time, these marks of even the abstract body-in-representation. The palimpsest practises the unrepresentable: the corporeal deracination upon which its final or uppermost discourse and its extant power are based.

So a painting which begins in the penal theatre of anatomy, as Rembrandt sketches the body of Adriaan Adriaansz., as it solidifies in death, comes to trace within itself the tropic outline of the modernity which is already establishing itself in place of the old substance of the flesh. In this twilight between the spectacle and the word it spans the historical reformulation articulated there, and measures out, in a fashion which is exemplary, the new design within which meaning and being alike will have to apprehend themselves. In its depiction of the older body, now extinguished, the painting can image the domination it quizzically celebrates, but it cannot strictly represent the subjectification which is its consequence. Inaccessible both to the Jacobean protocols of the body and to the conventions of nascent bourgeois realism, this subjectivity divided from itself can only be given to form, and then self-treacherously, in the textual devices by which the painting designates a concealed fissuration, naturalized by an overpainting which attempts to name identity but can never realize it. It inaugurates its trace of modern subjectivity by overlaying its corporeal poverty, but in the act of occlusion also marking, in the sheering between the strata of the image-text, in the unacknowledged passage from body to writing, the decentration, the instability, the absence from itself of the nominative subjectivity thus constructed.

If the authority, the mastery, of the new regime articulates itself in the name of science, the domination of the object, and if a certain realism is its proper aesthetic, there, to one side, in the margins of the text of the painting is the little subversion by which this structure of apparency and apprehension fails to fixate quite completely, where a slippage between identity and itself insists. Too late of course for Aris Kindt, whose names are scandalously many: but at least his body provided not only the occasion for the representation of this mastery, but also its anxiety.

If Rembrandt's painting is, then, the site of a corporal struggle, so too, although with a different outcome, is that other great anatomy lesson of the period: Marvell's 'To his Coy Mistress'. Each designates a crucial parameter for the modern body, and just as the painting in one of its movements makes the body text, so also does the poem, even as it unmakes the body it textualizes.

Had we but World enough, and Time,
This coyness Lady were no crime.
We would sit down, and think which way
To walk, and pass our long Loves Day.
Thou by the *Indian Ganges* side
Should'st Rubies find: I by the Tide
Of *Humber* would complain. I would
Love you ten years before the Flood:
And you should if you please refuse
Till the Conversion of the *Jews*.
My vegetable Love should grow
Vaster than Empires, and more slow.
An hundred years should go to praise
Thine Eyes, and on thy Forehead Gaze.
Two hundred to adore each Breast:
But thirty thousand to the rest.
An Age at least to every part,
And the last Age should show your Heart.
For Lady you deserve this State;
Nor would I love at lower rate.
  But at my back I alwaies hear
Times winged Charriot hurrying near:
And yonder all before us lye
Desarts of vast Eternity.
Thy Beauty shall no more be found,
Nor, in thy marble Vault, shall sound
My ecchoing Song: then Worms shall try

That long preserv'd Virginity:
And your quaint Honour turn to dust;
And into ashes all my Lust.
The Grave's a fine and private place,
But none I think do there embrace.
  Now therefore, while the youthful hew
Sits on thy skin like morning dew,
And while thy willing Soul transpires
At every pore with instant Fires,
Now let us sport us while we may;
And now, like am'rous birds of prey,
Rather at once our Time devour,
Than languish in his slow-chapt pow'r.
Let us roll all our Strength, and all
Our sweetness, up into one Ball:
And tear our Pleasures with rough strife,
Thorough the Iron gates of Life.
Thus, though we cannot make our Sun
Stand still, yet we will make him run.

Although the sharp pleasure of the poem corresponds to
an effect of power in one of its more spectacular forms – the
delight to be had from dismembering a woman's body – it is
still widely read as the light and conventional lyric of the
Renaissance libertine. There is no shortage of readings,
permitted by the ineffable distance which has come to
separate literature from all other discourses and all other
instruments of domination and resistance, that seek to
exhaust the meaning of the poem in the essentially
sentimental remark that it summons up, once again, the
ancient *carpe diem* motif, urging the beloved to amorous
delight before the rush of time wastes love, youth and beauty
alike. But this is a reading which stops short of registering
what it is no longer so necessary not to see: that the poem is
riddled by seventeenth-century discourse of the body. It is a
truncation which has been, no doubt, the product of the
hygienic attitude to the pleasures of the body of an age whose
moral ideology was, officially at least, more consolidated
than that of the poem's own historical time, a legacy of the
very process of corporal transformation and reinscription in

which the poem itself participates. Filtered through the post-Cartesian deployment of healthy discipline – which we shall soon evoke – and more locally through a certain propriety which can now be described in only the loosest of ways as 'Victorian', libertinage has come to signify aristocratic dalliance. But if so, then Marvell, who was not an aristocrat, was clearly not a libertine either: as de Sade reminds us, pleasure entails demanding effort. It is true, of course, that the poem devotes a third of its length, in that ornamented, richly surfaced verse which typifies so much Renaissance love poetry (although here it is taut and economical, its iconic quality as intellectual as it is sensual), to fabricating a luxuriant, semi-mythical world of courtly adoration among vast dimensions and slow temporalities. And this is the affective basis for the indulgent if mildly censorious reading to which the text is normally subjected. But the poem itself rejects that affect, for although the question of whether or not the idyll of burgeoning empires and sweet riches has yet begun to cloy in Marvell's hands remains moot, it is clearly a world that is not, but rather a poetic *topos*, condensed and lapidary, which the text quotes, with some triteness in the couplets, only for it to be swept at once aside. The more insistent temporality of what the poem encodes as the actual world, hastening on towards one consummation or another, soon breaks in on love's vegetative Golden Age and lays it to waste. For against the idyll and its affect, the poem is uncompromising in its sexual objectives, not to say its 'sexual politics': this is a poetry with operative purposes, designed to seduce. It has no romanticized disdain for tactics.

There might have been some comfort for the averted eye, or even for the kind of temperament which resists critical effects in literature, to read in the poem's transition from the gentle courtship of Love's fantasy empire to this new command of 'my Lust', with its vision of 'desarts' and 'ashes', a lament for a cultured and cultural fashion of loving. But there is no regret in the text. The poem cites a poetic ideology of courtship aestheticized and distantiates it, identifying on this side of the old kingdom a sexual urgency from which there is no respite, least of all a sublimatory one.

Here, on this side of the nostalgic fantasy, the poem says, love is not sacramental, it does not offer to redeem the lovers from the world, nor is it – for them or in itself – transcendent. On the contrary the poem twists away in another affective direction altogether, seeking in a reality principle, not the old empire but the new republic. The text ends neither in a sentiment of languishing indolence nor in one of satiated lust (either of which the libertine is frequently said to enjoy) but on an emphasis which is decidedly more rigorous. Goods are to be got, ultimately, by effort, and pleasures (if they are to be had at all, which the poem's final gesture does not guarantee) must be *torn* from inhospitable circumstances by struggle and amid conflict. The internal *milieu* of the poem is eventually one of 'rough strife', which, if it is a sexual metaphor is also in the historical context a political one. As the poem tends towards the future it reaches after objectives which will have to be wrested from life and from time, from history itself. This is, as Christopher Hill argued some time ago, an anti-epicurean ethic, and one which could be well described as militant and 'puritan', in its combativeness and its commitment to labour, if not actually in its emphasis on urgent sex.

In order to excavate the exact mode of the – contested – pleasure and presence of the body of the beloved, the poem must be read against the grain of the love-lyric into which the corporal discourse is imbricated; to decipher beyond what the poem says *of* its themes of love, sex and virtue (and beyond the interpretative chatter engendered by them), the discursive operations, hidden only by a certain kind of obviousness, *in its saying* of them, a rigorous literalism, perhaps even a nominalism will have to be the essential heuristic tool. For the literal body is in fragments: it is inscribed in the letter of the text as an inventory of parts, each in turn selected, treated and set aside: 'Thine Eyes', 'thy Forehead', 'each Breast', 'every part', 'the rest'. Marvell's 'beloved' is distributed across the text in discrete pieces. The body is scattered and diverse, the sum of its parts, although the totalization is never made, is greater – in textual extensiveness and sexual charge – than the whole: for it has no integrity, but merely a principle of the disconnectedness of its parts which belongs wholly to the discourse that articulates it according to a serial or spatial dispersal. It is appropriated and uttered within a syntax more remininscent of taxonomy than of the expectations of love poetry. Equally distant from amorous lyricism, what have been called the '*imagos* of the fragmented body' are identified by Lacan as the classic signs of what the discourse of psychoanalysis calls aggressivity: the torn flesh and the ruptured, separated organs, the shattered frame and the severed limbs insist in the speech, the fantasy and the dreams of the subject as the marks of an unrelieved violence as an inherent condition of its very subjectivity. These *imagos* haunt too the cultural text – in Lacan's example, the work of Bosch, where they are recomposed into new, fantastic, monstrous forms, and for us the spectacular cruelties of the Jacobean stage, and here, with a slightly different inflection, this 'love' poem. At this, other, level 'To his Coy Mistress' is the bearer of that discursive aggression which dissects the body it has made word; and doubly so because, like Rembrandt's *Anatomy Lesson*, the dynamics of its body are, historically speaking, complex, its status contested within the text. For Marvell's poem has not yet laid the spectacular Jacobean *imagos* to rest, although it is also evidence of the historical impetus towards allotting the body to a final obscurity. The struggle can be read in the modulation of the body through the text. The initial, and for the major part of the poem essential, condition of the body is still one of visibility. The text exhibits, and even in its brutal way – within the economy of violence the *imago* of the fragmented body discloses within the conventional lyricism – celebrates the body of the beloved in public view. The body is still recalcitrantly and defiantly on display, even if in a radically analysed form. It is still there to be seen, and is acknowledged openly as the object and site of desire. But in tune with an entire developing perception of the dangerous passionateness of the pre-disciplinary flesh, the text rounds on this first condition of the body of the woman, and having first torn it to pieces, not satisfied even by this act of violation, seeks to quell the restless anger of its own desire by consigning it to the darkness and silence of the 'marble Vault'. To still in death the Other of its own frustration.

The movement is, once more, from the spectacular corporeality of the Jacobean plenum to the corporeal extinction we have noted in Pepys, and which forms one moment of the modern body. But precisely because this is a transitional text, power over the body has not yet been wholly assimilated into its modern forms, the mode of sovereignty sought by *The Anatomy Lesson* in its depiction of the calm science of the bourgeois order. If Marvell's dismemberment owes something to the measured precisionism of the judicial torturer, as does Tulp's, nor have the incisions yet become wholly clinical. So that as that last cut which 'should show your Heart' offers to the enquiring gaze of the surgeons gathered round the table the chief of the vital organs, so it also displays that bloody pumping heart which was so often held aloft to one audience or another gathered at the foot of the public scaffold, dramatic or penal. If the progress of this fractured body through the text has science in it, if this text *is* a discursive surgery, the operation isn't only carried out in the name of a detached and scientific curiosity but belongs also to both of those other seventeenth-century theatres of cruelty. As we watch the cure become an autopsy, we are also spectators where the lover's caress turns into an act of Jacobean slaughter and where the king's wrath issues in corporal revenge. The discovery of the bleeding heart is the last act of both the tragedy of the blood and the terrible price of treason.

But if the text contests within itself the status of this body, its final tendency is towards the corporal situation of the modern body in its absent moment. It conceives for the vivid body a grave destination beyond sexuality and publicity. It cannot yet figure, as the Rembrandtian instance begins to, a new set of social and discursive relations which will reinscribe in healthy presence the new flesh, but must reduce the body utterly to a neutral dust: the least condition of the body, a sexlessness paradoxically counterpointed in the conceit of necrophiliac exploration, by the feeble sexuality

90

of the worms, of death's sterile chastity. The devastating punishment of the woman's 'coyness' which, even as it woos her, the text exacts in the very *form* of its courtship, decodes into the order of spectacular blood revenge, but the final gesture of the text's rendering of the body is towards another regime. It is to deliver the body into permanent incarceration in 'a fine and *private* place'. We are beyond the pleasure principle.

It will perhaps be labouring the obvious – although in a historical moment marked by such epistemic effort issuing on to so much mystificatory percipience, the literal and the obvious begin to require the most careful excavation – to suggest that whereas the dominant tendency of *The Anatomy Lesson* is towards the present aspect of the modern body, the reason that Marvell's lyric so vigorously ascertains the absent moment, its utter expurgation, is because of the gender as well as the sex of the body distributed across its text. Certainly it is *as body* that the woman is present to the poem, in the form, of course, of that absence. For if, as the Pepysian example suggests, a troubled, censored, sexed discourse is the characteristic of modern subjectivity, the woman, on the other hand, is without discourse. She does not speak, not even with an implied speech suggested by momentary pauses for response, or other hesitations, in the inexorable male voice which utters the poem. In a place which the poem addresses and labels 'Mistress', 'Lady' – woman – there is silence. The poem reticulates within itself and at its threshold a literary structure of speech and silence, an apparently full male discourse and an empty place, which it is necessary to encounter certainly as a power relation, and perhaps even the site of a political engagement.

When the voice designates the woman's silence as 'Coy' it is essentially as an incorporative gesture that it does so, the utterance gathering the woman into imputed complicity with its own discourse of love. There is a certain tantalized fascination, complementary to the aggressive fetishization of the parts of the body, with the reluctance of the woman who is cast at first as guiltless: at least in the seductions of the

91

fantasy empire, 'This coyness Lady were no crime'. But there is also something minatory, a threat of the potential violence – underpinned by the literal violence of the *imago* – latent in this apparently gentle appellation of the woman's passive resistance. Behind the initial banter of the lover's discourse and its ingenious persuasiveness is the implacable rattle of 'Times winged Charriot hurrying near', in the path of which what the male *persona* soon perceives in the woman's 'coy' reluctance as an artful refusal of sexuality comes to look more like a stubborn and destructive wilfulness, and her silence the sullen denial of an encratic speech not of persuasion but command. After all, Time is bearing down, and with it the entire weight and fury of the patriarchal tradition which, in the real republic, however much its ideology may mark out chastity as a proper register of femininity, none the less exists to secure the subordination of women. There is here a doubled structure of coercion operating behind the back of an apparent freedom, a strategy characteristic not only of the modern regime of gender but of the normal functioning of bourgeois domination as a whole. That the male voice must persuade and cajole rather than simply compel implies a right of refusal, but behind this indulgent male tolerance is the rage of a Pepys against the irrationality and delinquence of women; and here, in Marvell's punitive and finally morbid dissection, the Law offers to extract a terrible price for the woman's transgression of its desire.

Conceivably only another ruse of that same law would make us try to sustain an anti-reading of the poem, and thus to attempt to turn it against its own sexual fixing. But an analytic distinction can be forged between the male utterance of the poem and the text 'itself' (although they are empirically coterminous), constructing the text as radically distantiatory of the poem, and allowing us to apprehend, in spite of and at odds with itself, the poem's strategic and dominatory functions at work. The text as underside of the poem figures, in the woman's silent resistance, a refusal to enter into dialogue with the male voice and thus a declination of interpellation by its terms-setting, power-laden utterance;

a resistance which is quiet here because to respond is already to be ensnared, but which must be held instead as marking textually a mute limit of the penetrative capacity of the male voice; and silent because it must yet find its own proper discourse and fight out its essential campaigns elsewhere, on another terrain: it is the silence of Dora, who walked out. From this perspective, reading the poem from the side of what it is not, from a place which the poem determinately cannot see if what it does give speech to is to be said at all, the male voice can be understood as crying vaingloriously and even somewhat pathetically into a silence it doesn't notice. No actual 'woman' is listening, or, if listening, only negligently and with scorn. Unknown to itself, although marked in the text, the poem encounters an autonomy (albeit from the side of the poem a 'passive' one) of which it cannot conceive and certainly cannot give to discourse.

The gendered voice that *is*, however, given to subjectivity, like that of Pepys' discourse on the French text which has supplied the body as the object of a – frustrated – desire, revolves alone, and completely within the speaking of its own 'dialectic'. But there it constructs not only the woman's spoken absence but also, *sotto voce*, the only mode of her speechless presence it will admit. For however the silence which occupies the woman's place is read, it can never signify *for the poem* the existence of the human subject which is to be the key organizing figure of bourgeois culture, of its meanings and its texts. The woman is an objectified body at which speech is aimed, and which the poem organizes for the historical purposes at work here, but whose being is, so to speak, sub-discursive: dumb, reduced, corporeal matter. It is against this object-body that, even then, the violence of the poem is unleashed. But because of the historical ambivalence of the body in this compromised text, the gendered re-duction cannot be total: enough residual difference stemming from the older order – and illustrating, method-ologically, the *only* present value of the past: parallax – remains in its visibility to prevent this gesture being wholly victorious. The poem is after all a call for the consummation of the pleasures of the body: sex is its publicly avowed objective even if violence is its formal desire. The poem cannot tolerate the dangerous excess of the body it traduces, but just as so many Jacobean texts disintegrate under the twin drive to represent and destroy women, so this poem cannot wholly banish it either, and assign its dangers utterly to confinement. That, at least, remains minatory. Instead, as we have noted, the poem arcs away towards an *ideological* result which, while it has traces of the body in it – 'thy skin', through which, in textual mockery of the subjectivity denied the woman systematically by everything that has preceded it, 'thy willing Soul' sweats, at 'every pore' – none the less acts as an evasive bypassing of the discursive conflict which is thus historically – although not poetically – left in suspense; and effects, with a shift of grammatical number, a metaphysical fusion of the lover and the beloved, a mysterious solidarity which can then issue triumphalistically on to the ethical militancy of the last lines.

The success of the poem is in never having to face the text in history, so that beginning in the address of more or less polite courtship, it can end in protestant activism. It may turn out that the lover is the puritan's familiar. If so, a thing they will have in common is that each is variously committed, in a mirror-relation suited to the absence–presence thematics of an unhistorical culture, to a campaign for the measure of the body and its passions.

But if a reductive subjugation of the body is foreshadowed in Hamlet's desire for corporeal dissolution, illustrated in *The Anatomy Lesson*, practised vengefully in Marvell's lyric, and largely repressed as the underside of discourse in Pepys' text, this is not to say that the body is utterly evacuated from the bourgeois regime as a whole, and that *nothing* but a ghostly, troubling absence survives in what would otherwise be a realm of pure spirit. For all that the philosophical forms of bourgeois thought, and its literary criticism overwhelmingly, have aspired to such idealism and behaved on occasion as if decorporealized etherealism were a viable political instrument, this tactic only represents one side of the total strategy.

At the same time as bourgeois power rarefies the material in its search for the tranquil and tranquilizing ideal – the fable of the ascertainment of its own domination – it also, as its other side, issues onto a positivism of the object. It must master the body of the world in practice at the same moment and within the same gesture and purposes, as it de-realizes it in thought: not so much denying the world – which, on the contrary, it strives to dominate – as opening up that powering and powered division between body and soul, object and subject, which is the principle of its sexuality, its epistemology and its representation, and which in the widest sense designs the characteristic structures of the new culture.

Descartes is the unacknowledged legislator of this eventuality: at least unacknowledged in so far as his text is still so frequently thought of as purely – ideally and archetypically – *philosophical.*

But is the Cartesian text not a political anatomy too?

Certainly it often comes as a surprise to first-time readers to find, eventually, and after the absolute erasure of the body and all other 'corporeal things' in the instant of the *cogito,* that when Descartes has established the existence of God and then reconstructs the external world, the outcome is that long exposition in the fifth part of the *Discourse* of the structure of the heart and the circulation of the blood. Or that in a similar way the sixth, and last, of the *Meditations* is devoted entirely to describing, accounting for, and justifying the body. It turns out, against the odds of the erasure, that the health of the body is the highest good and the end of philosophy. Descartes tells us that his intention is 'to devote [his] whole life in the search for such a necessary science' as will allow us to 'free ourselves of an infinity of illnesses' (*D,* 79): and the last part of the *philosopher's* life is indeed spent in attempting to apply his method in order to derive from Nature 'rules in medicine which are more assured than those we have had up to now' (*D,* 91).

But despite the shock of the body's return to the philosophical text, let it be clear that 'rules' is the operative term, and that the heart of Descartes's text resembles but differs in its correspondence to the bloody organ exposed by

95

the last act of Marvell's loving dissection of his mistress just as that organ resembles and differs from itself. The Cartesian heart has already taken on the diagrammatic quality which corresponds to that of the representation of the hand in *The Anatomy Lesson*, a graphic and abstract delineation of the parts, organized now according to the categorical imperatives of knowledge rather than the sanguinary ritual of the old pain. Descartes's description of his own body is separative and itemized, like that of Marvell's object-woman – 'I perceived that I had a head, hands, feet and all the other members of which this body that I considered as a part, or perhaps also [terrible hesitation] the whole of me is composed' (M, 152) – but it is now the anatomy of a conception, to which the diagrammatic figuration is appropriate (and which thus produces the aesthetic anomaly in Rembrandt's image as it seeks phenomenal realism *and* the depiction of the concept at the same time, and issues onto – in discernible form for us – at least one of the antinomies of the new regime of representation). But if the abstracting gaze of science seeks a decorporealized body of and for knowledge this is not to maintain that, initially at least, it totally lacks sensuality. On the contrary, the reader of the *Discourse*, who is instructed 'to take the trouble, before reading this, to have cut open in front of them the heart of some large animal which has lungs, because it is, in all of them, similar enough to that of man' (D, 66), is then invited to reach into the cavity and touch in order to confirm the presence of 'the heat which one can feel there with one's fingers' and to ascertain 'the nature of the blood which can be known from experience' (D, 68). But here the sensual contact with the body is a desexualized, evidential encounter; and in practice it is only recommended to those 'who do not know the force of mathematical demonstrations and who are not accustomed to distinguishing true reasons from mere verisimilitudes' (D, 68). Strictly unnecessary, this tactile exploration is no more than confirmatory of the abstracted knowledge which is to dominate the discursive procedures of the modernity uttered here: the flesh is made to contribute, as a material,

96

to the science which is to dominate it.

This curious rehabilitation of the body, which the Cartesian text signifies in its closing pages, corresponds to what has been referred to earlier as the present moment of the new body – to distinguish it from the Pepysian discursive absence, or the Marvellian reduction to that morbid absence. Perhaps it would be better called the Other body. It is that positive body, no longer present 'in' discourse, but now, over there, an object of discourse; the body which presently – and at its best unequivocally – yields up in its modernity not a recompense of pain, but one of knowledge as the essential form of its mastery. Where Marvell's poem must tame its excess by ascription to deadly, obliterate privacy, as the pleasure principle reveals beneath itself the death drive against the passions of the flesh, Descartes must attend to the health of a body which is now to be disciplined and, according to a complex set of imperatives which should no doubt be referred to as 'economic', pacified, organized and prepared, ultimately, for labour. Its Calibanistic rebelliousness tamed, the Cartesian body is one subordinated to a hygienic and surgical science. In the double movement of inception of bourgeois modernity, at the same time as the body must be 'depassionated' and dispersed in an action of gendered degradation, so must it be reinscribed and positively charged as the bearer of a useful health. Perversely, the positive body becomes once more, as in Rembrandt's painting, the site of meaning, but in this contained and transcribed form. Almost subject, even, to a transubstantiation.

Suffering such a change the body can then be reconnected to the self. Having at first designated the essential I as composed only of thinkingness, the Cartesian text can even refer, eventually, to a mind-body composite as the total self. But this is achieved not in the fusion of one substance, although the intermingling of the body and the soul is near complete, but on the basis of the very separation which makes some provisional linkage possible:

And although perhaps (or rather as I shall shortly say,

certainly,) I have a body to which I am very closely united, nevertheless, because, on the one hand, I have a clear and distinct idea of myself in so far as I am only a thinking and unextended thing, and because, on the other hand I have a distinct idea of the body in so far as it is only an extended thing but which does not think, it is certain that I, that is to say my mind, by which I am what I am, is entirely and truly distinct from my body, and may exist without it. (M, 156)

The *problem* of the body is signalled in the attention this text must pay to it, but the recuperation of that problem consists not in a full reinstatement of the body in its old splendour: the 'unity' of I with it that Descartes posits is only maintained across a mutual, although not symmetrical, distinctness – a non-identity which is defined at last, significantly and *reasonably* enough under the historical circumstances, as a property relation: 'Nor was it without some reason that I believed that that body which, by a special right, I call mine, belonged to me' (M, 154). Object of knowledge and bearer of the spirit as – in Descartes's metaphor – the ship, the pilot, the positive body is re-admitted only in such subordinate function. It even remains signally outside that universality-essentiality structure which may be extrapolated as the self-appreciation of bourgeois culture as a whole and is certainly proper to the decisive instance of the modern soul. For where the reason of the mind is universal, the disposition of the body is always particular; where the soul is one (or as we should have to say after Freud, lives itself narcissistically in this presumed self-identity), the body is, as we have only too graphically seen, in Rembrandt and elsewhere, susceptible of radical division: 'if a foot, or an arm, or any other part, is separated from my body, it is certain that, on that account, nothing has been taken away from my mind' (M, 164). And where the soul is cardinally essentialized in its common sense, the body is only sensate in so far as God has seen fit to occasion a suitable liaison between it and the soul. Despite the notion of the composite, Descartes even fabulates an originary myth of the body as first-created, to which the rational soul, which cannot be 'in any way derived from the power of matter' (D, 76), is then added by God, not only spatializing but also producing a chronological sequentiality in the *difference* upon which the composition of the new body with the sovereign soul is in fact based.

Finally of course it is the externality of the body – in both of its aspects – to discourse itself that determines the subordination inherent in the body's reinscription within the structures of modernity. The Cartesian body is 'outside' language; it is given to discourse as an object (when it is not, in its absent moment, exiled altogether) but it is never *of* languaging in its essence. Indeed the body can now have no essence, not least because of this alienation from what the Cartesian text establishes as the constitutive centre of discursive practice. For Descartes the primary ground of the differentiation of men from the animals – and particularly from the imitative animals that are capable of uttering words and from the lifelike automata which could be made to do so – is that the parrots and the as yet merely mechanical fore-runners of Frankenstein's limit exploration of this argument 'could never use words or other signs, composing them as we do to declare our thoughts to others' (D, 74). While there is, for Descartes, a surprisingly societal register to this potentially communicational invocation of 'others', the determining figure is still none the less that of atomized interior constitution: it is in the rational soul of man that the capacity for productive semiosis is centred, the originating and constitutive source of a discursivity distinct from that of the mere words of the animals and the machines which themselves result from no more than the 'natural movements' of the body, achieved only in the disposition of the organs (D, 75).

This last asymmetry on which the manifest composite of the essential, discoursing soul and the positive but centreless body is founded is crucial because it is definitive of what, according to the ineluctable criterion, which the ruling culture will now valorize, of centration in, and mastery of, rationalist discourse, is now to count as legitimacy for the subjects thus simultaneously subjected and empowered. That this capacity for full and productive speech is forged by censored texts – both the Pepysian textualization of the subject and the Cartesian 'theorization' itself are, as we have seen, shaped around what must not be said (Descartes refers to this explicitly at the beginning of the sixth section of the *Discourse*) – cannot function for these texts themselves, as they are present to themselves, as anything more than a marginal irony, however critical it may be for us. It does nothing within the frame to hinder the work by which they fashion the self-sufficient density of the subject as the author of its own speech; and not simply as a work of description, but one of prescriptive structuration by which a radical inequality is written into the newly constructed taxonomy of subjects and objects of discourse. Although the marginal notations of the censorship may allow *us* to accede to a critical decomposition of the sovereignty and autonomy of the subject in beginning to undo the fixing of this apparency, and to see in this ostensible liberty the effect of a domination, the structure fashioned in and by these texts allows only of this pseudo-freedom of the subject and domination of the object: the soul constitutive of speech as its instrument and expression on the one hand, and the mute object at which discourse is targeted, on the other.

For the subject the positive body is thus reinstated to subjectivity in the place of silence exterior to language, a place it shares, of course, with Marvell's mistress. It is with an identical gesture that the modern structure disclosed severally in the texts we have been discussing excludes the body from the proper realm of discourse and simultaneously genders that very structuration, of which Marvell's lyric is both testimony and instance. For if the new regime in inaugurating itself deploys a pattern of speech and silence, a semiosis, in which the discoursing I is held to be constitutive, then it is clear that the designated woman is positioned extraneously to the constitutive centre where the male voice speaks. The woman is allotted to the place of the body outside discourse, and therefore also outside the pertinent domain of legitimate subjecthood. The silence in the place addressed cannot now be understood as an accidental and empirical feature of the poem, but as a historical delimitation. For the speech–silence semiosis which is modern textuality, or, as the phonocentrism of the modern would have it, subjectivity, depends as much on Marvell's lyrical-surgical assessment of the object-woman as it does on Descartes's apparently more detached and more purely philosophico-scientific delineation of that subjectivity 'as such'. In any case, the gendering marks the Cartesian text too, for when it defines the objectives as 'the general well-being of men', when this is inscribed in the letter of the text, we should take it at its word and refuse to reconcile ourselves to the fact that the last involution in the flickering substitutional procedure we are following here as the text readmits a kind of body, is to instate in the cleansed but distant place of Cartesian positivity not the absent female body of the poem, but one which is finally and unambiguously masculine. It is Aris Kindt who provides the flesh from which is elaborated by textual design the form and the gender of the corporeality which must now be the sovereign possession of every rational soul and every legitimate bourgeois subject. The Cartesian text brings the body back from what, in the moment of Marvellian 'lyricism', is the other place of the object-woman, overcomes the critical instability of the last redoubts of the old regime where, as we have suggested, so many Jacobean texts fragmented under the strain of taking the perilous body of the woman as their representational focus, and establishes, to its own satisfaction at the level of the fixation at least, the healthy male body as the only official vessel for lawful subjectivity. The price paid may be mechanism, but the danger averted is that of passion, womanhood, animality, dumbness.

To read the Cartesian text in this way is not therefore merely to cite a particular reflection of the medical history of the body – although this might have been unstable enough in respect of the normally philosophical reception of the

Discourse and the *Meditations* – but to locate it within a wider economy of mastery, to appreciate its effectivity in the construction not just of a personal body but of a novel body politic, mediated, in the first instance, by its representation. Despite the fact that such a difficulty could only exist on the basis of there being enough distance between representation and the represented for such an anxiety to appear, the epistemological 'problem' of the accuracy of a discourse-text's depiction of the real – and hence, according to the classical problematic, the doubt surrounding its purchase on, finally, power – can only be thought within a formation of knowledge which accepts this separation within representation as primary; without diagnosing it as historically constituted and constitutive. The historical effectivity – powerful, precisely – of the Cartesian text is to open the allegedly eternal gap between subject and object which will transfix philosophy, vitiate – latterly – politics, and even today infect those *radical* discourses which should otherwise regard such a luxuriously *philosophical* problem with studied negligence. Perhaps it is only if the traces of corporeality in the caesurae that define modernity can be apprehended as problems not for, but of, discourse that we shall be able to take a finally political measure of the domination exercised, as Althusser remarked, in 'the "simplest" acts of existence: seeing, listening, speaking, reading'. It is to this 'measure' that the last section of this essay will attend. But on the ground, in sum, of the political traduction which the Cartesian text effects. It legislates for an inner and alienate subjectivity and thus also calls into being the reduced and positivist body which bears on its flesh not the inscriptions of the penal instruments but the scars now, in sharper outline, of the surgical tools which are the practical arm of the regime of ideal knowledge which modernity establishes in contradistinction to, but tendentially dominatory of, the body of the material world itself. It is a body deracinated and then relocated. It is, shall we say, philanthropically rescued from the exactitude of the old corporeality (which must now appear, from the point of view of the new regime, as brute matter, once flagrant and sensationalistic but now thankfully subdued) and is then redesignated by modern discourse which, if not more scientific in the degree of precision of its technique than the older penal sciences of the body, none the less encodes itself as such: medical, knowledge-giving, epistemological. The once-unseparated ground of the previous body here gives way to the material and ideal separations of the modern which are exemplified as much by the marginal, excentred body of the Pepysian text as by the positive body of the regime of Cartesian health. For these liaisons, relational nexuses in a structure (rather, ultimately, than substantives) are articulated in the forms of knowledge which in turn articulate the field of division in which gendering and subjectivity can take effect as domination and appear as themselves *objects* of investigation. The mastery of the body on which subjectivity is predicated by these texts by no means depends wholly on the violent decorporealization of the flesh, but also on the equally aggressive solidification of the object-body and of the practical knowledges – discourses – which attend to its philosophical status, its psychic and physical administration, the organization of its sexuality and the definition of its gender. Even if that solidification is abstractly coded as analytic, diagnostic, diagrammatic, conceptual.

*   *   *   *

A seventeenth-century group portrait, a seventeenth-century lyric and a seventeenth-century philosophical alibi, each organized, knowingly or not, around the body, its dangers and its uses: the texts figure, in a *dispositif* of violence, valencies and conditions of modern corporeality, as in vengeful recompense the body is reduced simultaneously to the private residuality that haunts the discourse of the subject, and the positive object of a mastery as aggressive in the name of knowledge as the old sovereignty ever was in the exercise of corporal pain as its characteristic strategy. But if the old body stood at the centre of its culture as the word made flesh, the new body, in both its absent and its positive aspects, registers itself as flesh made word: the

103

body pressed back across representation and then rehabilitated within the model and the distribution of a mode of discourse that will only readmit the body at the price of its figuration in not, at last, speech, but text. Pepys has played such an important part here because of his exemplary displacement of the charge of the sexed body on to the sexed text, a move inherited by Freudianism whose scandal is not that it refuses the verbalization of the flesh – on the contrary – but that it will posit the arc of desire in the displacement itself. For this body, tensioned across its passages from positivity to absence and back to positivity (to death, in fact, and also, by return, to simultaneous abstraction and objecthood), can no longer stand at the *centre* even of its culture's self-identifications let alone at that of some more critical description of the versatility of its structure. From the point of view of the ruling culture, the body lies outside; and for criticism not only does the very dividedness of the modern body contain within itself the antitheses of presence and absence, positivity and denial, subjection and objectivity, which also characterize what Lukács was content to refer to as the 'antinomies' of bourgeois thought, but also behind these bipolar self-figurations of the culture, critique can glimpse, in the restless difference of the textuality of bourgeois society in its most unguarded phase, a complex set of displacements without stop or centre which replaces the old plenum and produces a body which is asymptotic rather than grounding, and an ideological ensemble which is relational rather than substantial. Not merely a structure of plus and minus, but a set of liaisons at once more holistic and more vacant than this binary simplicity; for it is in refraction and eccentric structuration that these relations may be apprehended and, critically decoded, in the instability inherent in the inevitable slippage between evinced bipolarity and the decentration itself. What is described by the new corporeality is a dispersal of discourse which must ever enter a hollowed world, launched from inside to outside, with nothing but an illusory, self-substantiating hope of arrival, and, conversely, without any security given in the stability of the place from

104

which it is dispatched. Bourgeois discourse in its typical form involves itself in the paradoxical self-contradiction that at the same time as it relentlessly embeds itself in the fixation of the integral and constitutive subject which is held in place against an ascertainable object-world, signification, representation and meaning must then become relational, figured across that gap between subject and object, and must always threaten, should power waiver and the slippage overcome the fixity, to devolve the actually constitutive, decentring play of presence-absence into the subject itself in the form of breakdown, and onto the world in the form of the dissolution of the naturalization of its apparency: to bring on, in other words, its own revolutionary vulnerability.

The entry and purchase of this instability has been referred to above as the metaphysics of death, which Hamlet articulates in its vacancy, which the Pepysian text elaborates discursively in its absentiation of the body, and which the dissections of Rembrandt, Marvell and Descartes each figure as they delve within in pursuit of both the extinction and the ascertainment of the external object. But perhaps it would be better to call it a metaphysics of death, not simply because of the evident violence of these texts, but because of the very structure of an absentiating mode of discourse which in reaching across the new gulf of representation – as it must now do in order to be discourse – must depend on the absence, the non-being or death, of the very object it seeks to designate. Discourse, substituting itself for the body-object, as the text is substituted for the flesh, is thus structured by precisely that morbid abnegation. It departs from itself in order to have something corporeal to represent – for in a positivist universe, without an object of knowledge there is strictly nothing to say – but in so far as it is constrained to operate this structure of separation it must set at a permanent distance the signs which are to be interpreted if meaning is to inhere. It founds itself on a gulf which is to a degree unbridgeable, and necessarily so for this discourse to function meaningfully at all. The interpretation becomes at best a kind of mourning for the object which it first calls into being and then abolishes. This necessary and fatal distancing of what the discourse apprehends or interprets is perhaps nowhere more ostensibly paradoxical than in the case of that knot of sometimes privileged discursive practices we call 'literature', which is still so frequently taken both as the repository of humane value and felt experience – 'life', in short – and as the extreme, the limit form of languaging as such, language as its most rarefied and its most concrete. At odds with the operation of a political analytics of discursive function, or even a hermeneutic, the problematic of literary referentiality standing in here for all discourse cast in this mode, bases itself by definition on the absence of the signified to which reference could in principle be made: a vacuity both in the 'primary' text, and in the commentary that doubles and shadows it. In this case the discourse which is known, unaccountably, as 'criticism' must engage a drive which is at root necrophiliac if, in being either a positive or an interpretative discourse on discourse, a twofold death of the celebrated object is at stake.

Nor is it only the death of the object which must underpin the logic of bourgeois representation. The slippage towards decentration of the structure, unless continually arrested by interpellation or cancelled by some wider solution, must also entail the suicidal denaturing of the subject which the decorporealized discourse defines. For when discourse crosses – in pursuit of the object or even in aimless 'self-expression' – the divide around the private place in which Pepys' and Milton's citizen in their civil 'liberty' write, so must it become as an object in the world over against the subject which in the fantasy of the fixation had sought first to create discourse and then to possess it, to mean in it and to control it – like Christ, both author of, and incarnate in, the word. But from the side of the divide where the subject is present to itself the essential modern fact of discourse must be its alienation into the public world, its entry there into the condition of an appropriable and distributed materiality and thus into a nihilation of the presence of the present voice which was apparently its starting point and content. Against the bourgeois mythologization of discourse as the transcription of the being of the originary subject, the other side of the same coin as the positivism of the object, is thus figured instead the departure of that discourse at every moment of utterance from the subject who can neither control its uses, destinations and meanings, nor remain present in it: as we have seen in Pepys and Descartes, not even the I that is spoken is the same as the I that speaks. Unlike the older settlement of body and being guaranteed within the single presence of the king, the modern equation of subjectivity with discourse, with textuality, contains within it the centrifugal tendency that, distributed among the structures of presence and absence, subject and object, public and private, state and civil society, risks marking that discursivity, the very essentiality of the subject, as separated and hollowed, and engendering a splitting between discourse as self-possession and discourse as self-alienation which would thus only inaugurate the presence of the subject in order immediately to effect an erasure of that presence.

Perhaps it seems over-interpretative, the effect therefore of self-contradiction, to suggest in this way that bourgeois representation, both in its surface fixation and in its underlying motility, tends, on the side of the object and of the subject, to death. Surely the instance of a radicalism, or perhaps a disgust, which in challenging the particular historical organization which is its antagonist, reaches over into a hubristic critique of being as such: an extravagance akin to that of those poor souls who think that their bodies are made of glass, or that they are kings and dressed in purple when really they are poor and naked – the mad people whom Descartes banishes from the text of philosophical and political legitimacy. Maybe so; but if so, then in the name of the critique of a historical organization – bourgeois modernity – which has itself covered its particularity by universalization, not just in thought but in something close to actual global domination, even arming itself with the capability of destroying the planet and ending history itself: the universalizing dream in its potential fulfilment. But if it is commonplace today to remark that the word absentiates the thing it names, that the letter killeth while the spirit, it is also said (although this usually in other quarters), gives life, less frequently is it held that as the aphorism is itself pronounced in language, a hierarchy of powers rather than an equality is articulated by it, if not actually a cynical subterfuge in the promise of an illusory autonomy of the spirit from the violent letter. Ever since the later Freud, who, albeit unhistorically, identified the death drive as the principle not only of culture but of 'life' itself, it has been difficult to sustain the dejection which could see in this twin if unequal campaign for life on the surface and in that, inherently, for death, a governing unconscious motif, the cybernetics even, of an entire historical epoch, both in its wider encratic structure and in the apparently interior organization of its speaking and writing. But that is what is at issue now, in the structure, in the necessarily suicidal self-alienation of the subject whose integrity is in any case factitious, and in the murderous or elegiac dynamics of the interpretation of the object, functioning severally and together as instances and allegories of bourgeois discourse as such. For power in its modern form exists not simply in that external violence which the state can offer to its population, but also in the liaison of *that* power with the interior dividedness, the self-aggression of the subjects the state interpellates as the supports of its apparently exterior control. Not just a bureaucratic, a propagandistic or an armed power out there, but power in the form of the violence that intersects with the discourse, the gendered textuality of the subject, with the poignant languaging which the Cartesian text makes essential; nor just the threat – atomic now and total – which subdues from without and, *par excellence*, in the loss or the threat of loss which such a power to destroy disseminates, but also in the interiority where it has ever pre-intervened, insinuating itself within the subject at the very moment of its constitution. 'Is there anything', Descartes asks, somewhat querulously, 'more intimate or internal than pain?' (M, 155). It is precisely the intimacy of that pain, the mark of a violence which is structural to the modern subject and no doubt largely unconscious, that separates the particularity of this historical form of domination from others. Here, in the subjectivity of this subject, in the narrative languaging which we have seen to be its form, is the constituting introjection of the morbid aggressivity which is the shadow and, taken as the record of a historical structuration, also the progenitor of the other violences reaching from the existential detail up as far as the nuclear oppression itself.

The socio-historical trope of narrative here achieves an unexpected revenge on its cultural origin and purpose because it too constitutes discourse in absence. We have already noticed, in the forms variously disclosed by the Pepysian and the Cartesian texts, the construction of modern subjectivity in the transactions of, if not simple narrative, at least, narration, the narrationality by which – discourse preceding presence – the writing I finds and describes its being in a continual if disembodied text. And in this too there is a double absence, a twofold negation. For as the text becomes the body it thereby kills (and at the same time inscribes – even if largely ignorant of this too, in its Pepysian blindness – *that* absence within itself) it also describes a passage through time by virtue of which the seemingly eternal present moment of narration must distance along the line of its narrative both the point of departure from which it conceives itself as stemming, and the destinatory telos – in either anagnorisis or apocalypse – towards which it strikes out. The narrative is a 'chronological' absentiation, morbid thus in respect both of its imagined origins and its actual starting point, and equally negatory – although in this register 'transcendentally' – in respect of its goal (for if the destination is to be a goal it must also be, at any moment before consummation, absent, and even to achieve it would be in any case to terminate the narrative and kill off its dynamic). Hollowed and powered by the censored desire of the body which Marvell, Pepys and Descartes variously and perversely disclose, the dispersal of this narrativity must too encounter a slippage towards inherent impossibility of fulfilment linked to the instability of the subject-object fixing. The absence of the beginning and the end, like that of the body, is no merely empirical lack which could in principle be filled, if only there were world enough and time – a sufficient history – but a structural principle of this discoursing subjectivity, a very condition of its discoursing. Bourgeois representation and epistemology alike must mourn in the unconscious recognition of the unattainability of the ends and the permanent loss of the origins which they must nevertheless figure to themselves at the level of the fixation, the naturalization, the apparency, as present beginnings and full objectives. Like Spinoza's ardent life, which Macherey translates into an allegory of fictive languaging, the discourse must search in restless pursuit of an imaginary goal which it will never reach because the lack of its indefatigable, if subterranean, desire is precisely the apparatus of the quest.

If displacement and absence, the lack which is desire, the aggression which is a certain love, the emptied presence which had been once the old body are indeed structural to the new regime, then the death drive, which we have seen supplanting the pleasure principle in Marvell's lyric, and witnessed in the fatal virulence of Rembrandt's depicted and Descartes's textuated science, is not only a foundation of the new power but also its unknown objective. What we are constrained to regard as the culture's love and its knowledge, its gendering and its representation, meet in the unstable liaison of terms and relations which are, behind the fixation, at play in these texts and their deathly reduction of the body, and there provide the motive for the metaphysical fantasy – bourgeois death unknown to itself – which seeks if not centration, at least a stop of the culture's meanings: a closure otherwise impossible because of the very decentration which with its absentiating and narrativizing discourse inaugurates, and which must then be contained or even extinguished. Never strictly immobile in its apparently dichotomous but practically polychotomous deferral, the drive to domination and ascertainment – to realistic speech – could only ever

110

achieve the tranquility of the adequate fixing it aspires to in a more widely distributed absence, a death which is hence no merely adjectival or contentual property of the textual dispositions and discursive techniques we have seen at work in these seventeenth-century texts, but also inevitably the general goal of the modern culture of domination. In this sense the death wish, of which nuclear weapons are now the instrument and the manifestation, is in a strong form intrinsic to the modern discursive regime. A nuclear dénouement – apocalypse and, in the sense of the consummation of knowledge, anagnorisis – would secure the no more than felicitous conclusion in an instance of punctuality which bourgeois discourse is committed to seeking both as the imaginary, consolidating end, and also the unacknowledged drive, of its self-generation. Only in that final solution would the epistemic and sexual voiding which evacuated the bourgeois body from the bourgeois soul ever be allayed. The desire – let it be suicidal – for a finality, a plenitude of arrival – which must shape itself as the most complete absence possible – is the secret aspiration of this discursive register. And a suicide hardly more poignant for the fact that it doubles death over death in so far as even the satisfaction of the conscious project of bourgeois discourse entails its own death when to regain what was lost or to find what is sought would deprive it, if only in fantasy, of the lack which is its motive force. When previously could power in either its desire or its satisfaction destroy the world? But that must be its aim: to find in a general catastrophe, the devices of which bourgeois science in a direct line of descent from Descartes, as many have argued, has now provided, the end of all desire, of every discourse and narration. In this eventuality – only nameable as such by dint of a certain stoic will to irony – the hollowing would finally be filled, the absence supplied, and the slippage arrested, by a last erasure of the doubled architecture of presence and absence that describes both the 'inner' structure of bourgeois subjectivity-in-discourse and its 'outer' articulation. In this closure of the decentration – for which the political will probably exists – peace would finally have come . . . as the remains of the earth cool. The narrative would have been ended, and the last full stop put at the end of the otherwise diacritical history of the human species.

And let us not detect in this the banality that we all desire death, nor even that desiring death is the principle of our life (although both these formulations disclose in their different ways something fundamental), but that bourgeois 'society' is, in its structure and its distribution, gendered, morbid and atomic. The tragedy and necessity of such a domination that has committed itself, perhaps irredeemably, to the powerful if unstable strategy of simultaneously equating and separating identity and discourse are that it must manufacture such identity at all – that it must organize across its text a *gendered* subjectivity, produce the body as no more than a breathing simulacrum, and then desire a healing in global destruction.

MEN
WITH
GLASS
BODIES

Dr Nicolaas Tulp, surgeon and representative of the civil authority, anatomist and frequent office holder in the bourgeois government of Amsterdam. But also a general practitioner who, like Freud, left his case-histories, the *Observationes*, where the body is made text, and in which one of the patients is constrained to spend a winter in bed suffering from the insight that his bones were made of wax and would buckle if he stood up. The sick man was a painter to whom Tulp refers in a way that suggests it was Rembrandt, the most prolific producer of self-portraits ever, who was obsessed by the story of Samson and Delilah – that narrative of symbolic castration and the treachery of women – and whose first important canvas depicted Tulp's magisterial dissection of the executed criminal Aris Kindt. At which Descartes was probably present; anatomist himself, philosopher and legislator for modern subjectivity, who, meditating by the stove, considering strangely whether his body exists, uses the wax that is to hand to prove that corporeal objects have no consistency or essentiality but extension in space. And Caspar Barlaeus was almost certainly there at the dissection too, a leading intellectual and noted neurotic, who wrote poetry in praise of Tulp's dissection of Kindt, and dared not sit down for fear that his buttocks, which were made of glass, would shatter.

While in England, their brothers. Hamlet calling on his flesh to melt. Marvell, Member of Parliament, who let aggressivity write in his poem. And Milton and Pepys: each committed in their different ways to inexorable textuality; riven by equivocal desire. A revolutionary poet and censor, who also wrote a *Samson*, and a secret diarist narrating himself and his world in private. Both eventually blind....

But these are anecdotes and in some respects improbable, or at least not susceptible of proof. Surely not worth serious historical attention. And yet is there not something at once risible and haunting about a poet of the bourgeois class who thought that his body was made of glass (for Descartes, of course, strictly a madness); or salutary in an image of the public dissection of a man who had no respect for the law? Or revealing in men driven blind by writing? When we

115

consider these conditions in the representatives of a historical order, is there not some reflection to be made on the rationality and freedom in the elaboration of which the period is said to have made important advances?

Then do these fragments not begin to figure the outline of a historical fable, even a structure: at the foundation of our own epoch a conjunction of themes and powers which it is still ours to live, and if enough time remains, undo, today?